UNITED IN INSPIRATION

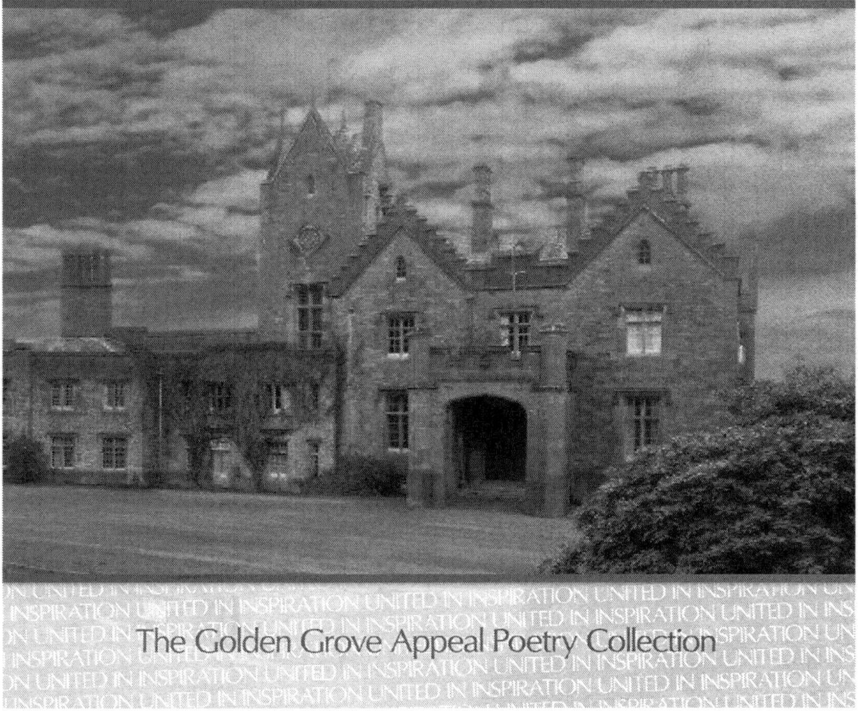

The Golden Grove Appeal Poetry Collection

Edited by Jonathan Fisher

First published in Great Britain in 2010 by:
Forward Poetry
Remus House
Coltsfoot Drive
Peterborough
PE2 9JX

Telephone: 01733 890099
Website: www.forwardpoetry.co.uk

All Rights Reserved
Book Design by Tim Christian
© Copyright Contributors 2010
SB ISBN 978-1-84418-553-5

Foreword

Here at Forward Poetry we are delighted to be able to help Golden Grove Appeal. We decided to team up with the charity, inviting you to send us your poems for this unique anthology from which we will donate 10% of the sales.

Golden Grove Appeal was founded by Kevin Richards, an ex-combat medic who saw the need for this much-needed facility in Wales. The charity hopes to purchase the Grade II listed mansion near Llandeilo, situated within one hundred acres of a beautiful country park, for use as a treatment facility for our armed forces personnel and veterans, who are suffering from PTSD (post traumatic stress disorder) and to provide convalescence. At present there is no such facility in Wales.

The charity have been given a short period of time to raise the required cost of purchase and the fund-raising continues in earnest. The tenacity and determination of the charity and its fundraisers has been inspirational to us at Forward Poetry and we are very proud to be involved in helping them. We are also extremely grateful to our amazing poets for their hard work in making this collection possible.

For further details please contact
www.goldengroveappeal.com

Golden Grove Mansion
Healing the Wounds

Contents

Betty Glover	1
Anita Maina Kulkarni	1
R S Parks	2
Pickle Lilly	3
Glenys Allen	4
Mike Subritzky	5
Grant Bayliss	6
Michele Amos	7
Lavinia Bousfield	8
Rosalind J Lee	9
Valerie Thorley	9
Josephine Jenkins	10
Linda Saunders	11
Richard Morris	11
Michelle Wright	12
Alan Mayes	13
Angela Cole	13
Joanne Ross	14
Terry Powell	15
Goblet Boodles	16
Poppy Harding (13)	16
Kent Brooksbank	17
Margaret Whitehead	17
Helgi Öpik	18
Roger N Taber	19
David M Walford	20
Bethan Walters	22
Jane Vickers	23
Linda Hearne	23
Suzy Turner	24
Mike Silkstone	25
Heather E Cook	26
Gary Maeslan	26
Jim Kimpton	27
Safia Siddique (14)	27
Iago AP Llewellyn	28
Felix Erasmus	29
Jeanette Hopkins	30
Sylvia Hughes	32
Lorraine England	33
Jill Govier	34
Michael Kwadwo Poku	35
Richard Jones	36
S R Hurley	37
Gael Nash	37
William Birtwistle	38
Anne Anderson	38
Patricia Stone	39
J M Crook	39
Christine Williams	40
Rosie Plimmer (13)	40
Irene Hall	41
Carla Stokes	42
Pauline Uprichard	43
Kathryn Wilkins	44
Sali Jones (13)	45
Daphne G Davies	46
Victoria Moulson (13)	46
Jane Margaret Isaac	47
Raven Pal	47
Elin Hopkins (13)	48
Kate Jasperse (13)	48
Rosie Plimmer (13)	49
Sinead Murphy (13)	49
Adam Reaney (14)	50
Ffion Caines (13)	50
Christopher Head	51
Ryan Jones (13)	51
Tom Cooze (13)	52
Mathew Jones (13)	52
Joe Leslie (13)	53
Sierra Gaffney	53
S M Thompson	54
Charlotte Beaumont-McAllen	55
Ritam Goswami	56
Wendy Shone	57
Rachel Sutcliffe	58
Daphne Cornell	58
Castallaman	59
Robert Black	59
Tessa Paul	60
David Sawyer	61
Alasdair Sclater	62
E Meletor Smith	63
Christopher R Slater	64
Jan Kerntiff	65
Ruth Tomkins	65
Beryl Henshaw	66
Norman Bissett	67
Paulette Francesca Sedgwick	68

Paul Kelly	69
Norman Biggs	69
Rhodri Williams (17)	70
Adrian Yates	72
Kate Miller	72
Mary Howcroft	73
Debra Ayis	74
George Carle	75
William Ross	76
Robert Main	77
G B Taylor	77
Anton Leslie	78
Robert Wynn-Davies	78
Helen Round	79
Sian Boissevain	80
Angie Davies	80
Robert John Ponting	81
Vivian Barlow	82
Janet Starkey	83
David J King	84
Noele Mackey	85
Fariah Rahman	86
Maureen Cole	86
William Meechan	87
Derek Gealy	87
Rebecca Farish	88
Siwla Virago	89
Jackie Domingo	90
Catherine Fleming	91
Florence Davies	92
E Evans	93
Jeanne Evans	94
Pat Gealy	94
Adwoa Asiedu	95
Doris Steere	96
Brinda Runghsawmee	97
Penny Gillman	98
Amanda Griffith	99
Sue Harries	100
Hilary Sauvarin Cackett	100
Margaret Edge	101
Ann Holland	101
Andrea Wren	102
Rebecca Taunton	103
Averil Fairey	104
Yvonne Brunton	105
Claire Morris	106
Trevor Foster	106
Hannah Hall	107
Barbara Lambie	108
Michael Lee Johnson	109
Kal Elias	110
Beverly Maiden	111
Sylvia Quayle	112
Vicky Stevens	112
Christine Weatherley	113
Philip Anthony Amphlett	113
Philip Ellis	114
Gaynor Morris	115
Lyn Lifshin	116
Samantha Williams	116
Jade Louise Piggott (16)	117
Abigail Donoghue	117
Dorothy Moody	118
Cecilia Jane Skudder	118
David Anderson	119
Barbara Rees	120
Scribbler	120
Frank Tampin	120
Yasmin Abukar Ahmed (15)	121
Suzanne Harding	122
Judith Roberts	122
Colin Jones	123
Maria Dixon	124
Stephanie Rees (10)	124
Neil Young	125
Jack Watson (13)	125
Helen Smith	126
Pam Mills	126
Edwin V Atkinson	127
Shirley McDonnell	127
Natasha Joan Dono (15)	128
James G Ryder	129
Joanne Lutwyche	130
Glenys M Bowell	131
Andrew Gruberski	132
Clare Todd	132
Donna Louise Salisbury	133
Tracey Davies	133
Arfon Williams	134
Lynda Ann Green	135
Ron Constant	136
Tara NíBhroin Byrne	137
Arun Budhathoki	137
Christopher J P Smith	138
Claire-Lyse Sylvester	139
Amanda Crowden	140
Ian Rae	141
Sandra Moran	142
Richard Jones	144
Eirlys Jones	144

Gillian Todd	145
Gary K Raynes	146
Michael James Ryan	147
Isolde Nettles Mackay	148
Helen Richards	149
Jane Green	150

The Poems

Faith

Faith, you're a friend in a million
That no one could ever replace,
A friend who is thoughtful and caring
In a million and one special ways.
We may have a laugh or a chuckle,
A moan and a groan sometimes too,
But whether it's sunshine or raining
Your friendship will always shine through.
Good friends are but few in a lifetime,
The good times and bad times we share.
So I write this poem with the knowledge
Of a friend who will always be there.

Betty Glover

Too Early For Revealing

Startling is the sunlight that wraps itself around revelations
as they turn back and stare at me full in the face.
Coloured chintz embodies the wind's demeanour
but only becomes unsettled once or twice while wafting in and out,
staying largely calm and unruffled. The rocking horse creaks
and the soft, cushioned chair rocks, idling its time for free
and free from the inertia it has grown tired of.

I am held captive as my thoughts engulf me,
forcing me to listen while I am still cocooned in the covers
like heavy webs; their cloying sticky threads, like iron
bars weigh me down and I feel a panic. Brainstorms hover,
and a deluge ensues, but there is no shelter despite
the overwhelming prison I sink ever further into, hoping
I can fall out the other side quite dry and unsullied.
I doubt this as I dig in the mire at my unshackled revelations.

Anita Maina Kulkarni

Carnival Of Volunteers

Didn't someone once sing . . . living is easy with eyes closed . . . ?
Dust, f*****g dust everywhere . . . in my clothes, my socks, my eyes . . . my f*****g soul.

If there *were* a God, an Allah, he wouldn't place me here, killing or being killed,
The game is the same each day, it's easier if you think it's not real,
No . . . more than that . . .

It's not real, it's not real, it's not real, it's not real . . .

But it is . . . *you* know it is and so do *I*, we *both* know I killed men today,
I will kill more men tomorrow, and the day after that,
I kill to not be killed, apparently.

Some days I am merely the puppeteer,
I pull the strings, which animate my soulless body,
Didn't someone once sing . . . I've got soul, but I'm not a soldier . . . ?

Why can't I bring myself to look at photos of home?

The fastest frustrations come as I pick up this uniform . . . this disguise,
The slower, more painful, come when I see them stare in fear,
Stare at me, this *protector,* walking their streets, smiling at their children,
Didn't someone once sing . . . killing in the name of . . . ?

I am stuck in this carnival of volunteers, one day I will wake,
It's not real, it's not real, it's not real, it's not real . . .

R S Parks

Golden Grove

Once upon a yesteryear
I could see a building
A mansion in fact, to be exact
A mansion so golden
They called it Golden Grove
A mansion - that was a place of safety
Helping the wounded, the injured of the bloody war
Healing the wounds
Today, the present, the future
That Golden Grove is no more
That mansion is wounded, injured, hurt and empty
History gone forever
Today we still need to fight
Fight as might we can
To get yesteryear today
To bring back the mansion back to its former glory
Come on fight the good fight
Come on Golden Grove
Your future is in our hands
Let's get it together
For Golden Grove.

Pickle Lilly

To My Unborn Child

Soon I will welcome you, my little girl or boy,
Though the waiting months at times seemed long,
they were always filled with joy.
I've watched your growth impatiently, your little life I've felt,
Through movements slight, then stronger,
from the womb wherein you dwelt.
When you arrive in this world of ours, the season will be spring,
The most wonderful time of any year for every living thing,
But this year the birds will sing sweeter,
The trees wear their brightest green,
the sun's rays feel much warmer,
and the flowers the most beautiful ever seen.
And now you too will blossom forth,
but a richer flower from above.
Your earthly life will be ever guided,
your years filled always with tender love.
Pray for the wisdom and the strength with which to guide your life,
Along the path the future holds of happiness and strife,
Some day I will tell you of the wondrous months we shared,
Whilst your spirit and your body were tenderly prepared.
But my eager heart awaits you with abundant love and joy,
So welcome soon to this happy home, my baby girl or boy.

Glenys Allen

Comrade Darlington MIA

To me, you were never a MIA
I know exactly where you are
in your shallow red dirt grave
just outside the wire
where those Fire-Force guys
burned and buried you.

To me, you are never missing
I see you every other night
or the next night, or the next
somewhere between the darkest hour
and the blackbird's morning call.

We never speak you and I
you can't, you're already dead
with limbs setting grotesquely
and eyes wide open and clouding
while I pour my water bottle over
your blood-stiffened pockets
and search for an identity.
Ah yes, I have it.
His name is Comrade Darlington.

(MIA = Missing In Action)

Mike Subritzky

My First Hero

Before Sinatra
Before Muhammad
Even before the love
Of the female form 'with colour'
My first hero
Already long dead
Captured the imagination
Of an obsessive child
And paraded their greatness
In print

A life unmatched
In incident
Was ferociously read
And remembered
Knowledge became the key
Is this destiny?
This monologue recorded
Born to a lord
A history of privilege
Courageously patriotic
Warmonger
Artist
Statesman
Canonised

Is this what excited
A naïve child
Tales of war
Of bravery
Beyond the line of duty
Or did the rhetoric
Strike a chord
The undeniable
Desire to

Defend the common man
At all cost
A resolute resounding
Orator
A trademark
For a generation
Is this perhaps the answer
Probably
But behind those incredible
Motivating speeches
That even now
Bring your neck hairs
To attention

England's greatest man
Victorious in gesture
Unyielding in the face
Of defeat
Perfectly timed
Our finest hour
And conquered
The tyranny
Of Hitler

Grant Bayliss

Gentle Spirit

(Written in July 2003 for my horse, Maisie,
who had a very bad accident the year before)

I saw your pain, your body ripped and torn,
No hope, they said, already weapons drawn,
You spoke to me in volumes higher than the trees,
You spoke to me in whispers softer than a summer breeze;

You told me I must let you try,
You asked me not to let you die.

With your eyes you spoke to me
In shades of brown and burgundy
With your heart you told me this,
In rhythms gentler than a kiss.

Time and patience you said were needed
With your eyes you gently pleaded
How could I reject your cry,
Let your brave and gentle spirit die?

You took your trust and in my heart you laid it
My beautiful girl, I'm so glad you made it . . .

Michele Amos

Remember Them
(I dedicate this to all our brave servicemen and women)

They all met up at Rubery Legion
On this cold day in November
To go down the street proudly
Fallen comrades to remember

Men and women in uniform
Some with medals on their chest
And some were pushed in wheelchairs
Paying homage to comrades laid to rest

The band played loud and clear
As they all marched along their way
All thoughts of what those brave men gave
For the peace in this land today

People stood and watched as they passed by
With flags and banners held with pride
To the memorial service they did go
To honour men, and women who died

By the church with heads held high
As the wreaths were laid upon the ground
On this cold November day, they did sing
With people gathered all around

Then in the church to sing and pray
The losses are deeply felt on this day
We will remember brave men and women
All over the country this Remembrance Sunday

Marching back to Rubery Legion
Wreaths and crosses on the ground they lay
Together we will remember them
Praying for world peace on this poppy day

All who have been badly injured now
We will give our love and care
Today our thoughts are of those
Who we loved, and held so dear

Lavinia Bousfield

Snowy Days

This takes the biscuit -
to ask me to write a poem
about snowy days.

When the sun
spirals into spring
tulips open into kisses.
Crocus, snowdrops
rise through the pansies.

It's a fallacy:
the jargon of snow,
the blanket of winter,
the harvest of souls.

It all melts away,
every sludge drop,
each leftover ledge.

The dragon's breath
comes: Ah, how it comes,
the tender quixotic.

Rosalind J Lee

Evening Birdsong

Sitting quietly as April dusk descends
No TV, radio nor noise to distract
The silence is broken by the
Heart-rending melody of songbirds
In the garden, in the distance
This final burst of beauty
Cutting into the chilly evening air
Will the songbirds be there tomorrow?
These birds that made my day
Will they repeat the message for me
Of what we can miss
When surrounded by noise?

Valerie Thorley

Adoption, A Mother's Memories

I have a room inside my head, that's full of memories,
Some days, I sit alone in there, just turning over leaves.
Some days, I look in through the door and glance upon a page,
The pictures that come flooding out, just fill me with a rage.

I remember all those years ago, the memories never fade,
I was alone and pregnant and very much afraid.
'You'll have to go away,' they said, 'some place where you're not known
And give it for adoption, and come back here alone.'

For me, a lonely childbirth, with strangers round my bed,
No smiles or words of welcome, for the little babe I had.
Somebody else would take my child, and have her for their own,
For me there would be emptiness and heartache, all alone.

I had her for such a little time, the days were soon all gone,
And I had to turn and walk away, from the little girl I'd borne.
I held her for the last time, I wished I could have died,
My arms would soon be empty, I cried and cried and cried . . .

No more tears, or words of comfort, to help to ease the pain,
It wasn't to be mentioned, or talked about again . . .
They thought that I'd forgotten, because no words were said,
But they couldn't hear my baby . . . crying in my head . . .

I wonder if they love her, or when she laughs or cries,
I wonder if she's walking yet? What colour are her eyes?
And when she's growing older, what will her future be?
Is she happy and successful? Does she ever think of me?

By chance, I'd heard a certain name, that I should not have known,
But it gave to me the knowledge of where my child had gone.
One day, one day, I'll find her and my heart's been aching so,
I dearly long to see her face and I can wait no more . . .

It wasn't easy searching, it was against the law,
But Fate had given me the key, to open up the door.
Over long weeks I waited, until the phone rang one day,
'I'd like to come to see you,' I heard a strange voice say.

The meeting with my daughter - something words cannot express,
After all the years of longing, such joy! Such happiness!
I've been so lucky finding her, how will our story end?
At least my long-lost daughter, can be, please God, my friend . . .

A word to other mothers, who'd search as I have done,
They're still someone else's daughter, or someone else's son.
You can't undo the past, you know,
What's done . . . is done . . . is done . . .

Josephine Jenkins

Killing Time

A kind of scallop-cum-flying saucer
is how I imagined it, walloping
out of a sky of fire. On his knees again,
scrabbling around for his glasses in the mire,
the rest of them bent double but still running,
is how he told it, and the shell thudding down
beside him, *this near!* - but a dud.

He never spoke of what he saw; he shut
remembrance in some inward vault,
only releasing that stroke of fate
which spared him at seventeen. To enlist,
he lied about his age, but soon in France
witnessed truths few would tell, or forget.
The lost numbered millions, leaving only names
to blister the stonemasons' palms.

By not one but a thousand near misses
he must have come through, with both legs
even after frostbite. No bedtime stories of horror
or heroics, though he told me how they raced lice
in the dugouts to kill time - as now his great grandsons
(who owe life to his luck) dodge bombs
on Gameboys, deadly with their ray-guns.

Linda Saunders

Take Time

Take time to look around and notice what is good
Take time to talk to loved ones and treat them like you should
Take time to smile at memories and laugh a little too
Take time to be polite and others will be too
Take time to take some time, relax and have some fun
Take time to feel the warmth and tingle of the sun
Time is precious to us all, enjoy it while you may
Embrace the wonder that it brings, each and every day.

Richard Morris

Waiting
(Dedicated to all who fight and their families)

Staring at the kettle
Thinking a watched pot never boils
She waited
China teacups sitting
Impatiently in cream saucers
Viennese slices melting

Minutes passed
Then an hour
Then two
As she waited
For him to return

Dogs barked
Neighbours came and went
Clocks ticked on
Normality seemed obscene
As she waited

Photographic reminders
Stared out at her
Last Christmas captured
When he'd returned
Slowly she rose
Going through the motions

Putting away China teacups
Removing Viennese slices
As she accepted
That he would not return

Michelle Wright

Home

I dreamt whilst I was away
to return home to a family nest
I would hope and I would pray
to be welcomed and caressed
with a safe secure place to stay

now I feel so heavenly blessed
to be removed from the disarray
my pals were simply just the best
for their bravery I shout, 'Hooray!'
I'm home but I'll not forget the rest
left to do official duties which they obey
my body and soul have been hard pressed
vivid memories when I'm old and grey

peace and tranquility is now my quest
miles from the hostility and affray
for life I now have a new zest
I'm going to live for today
have fun, excitement and jest
what more can a retired dog say

Alan Mayes

A Place

Am off to a lonely place
Where no one can see my face
Am in a room
Where nothing is there
How tearful I may just be
I just can't decide
Decide where I should be
In a happy place
Or in a sad place
Only I can decide
Of which place to go.

Angela Cole

Soldier Boy

What do most people think
When they see you proudly dressed in pink
Crocs, with T-shirt to match?
They must think I've bagged a strange catch

'Silly Grandad,' the children shout
As you joke and lark about
Youthful, playful, without a care
Age betrayed only by your grey hair

The women standing by the door
As couples smooch on the dance floor
Are flattered when you take their hand
And start cavorting to the band

The regulars in your local pub
Like a tight-knit and closed club
Open up, emerge from the dark
When you throw away a flippant remark

What they don't see, behind your joy
Is the young, raw, soldier boy
Life wasn't always such a laugh
Leaving home at fifteen and a half

For you, your views of life were cast
On the streets of Belfast
Your inner self really took root
When you found a foot, still in a boot

Or helped the Cyprus invasion end
But in the process lost a friend
Oh, there were good times too
That shaped the man who now is you

To the ladies you were rather partial
The reason for your court martial
Was simply being out of bounds
When to meet a young lady you left the ground

And you saw the world, if through soldier's eyes
And you sometimes basked beneath blue skies
On Malta's beaches, Sardinia's shores
There is more to army life than chores

But when people now see you play the fool
And judge you by some common rule
They little see both the pain and pride
That from the world you've learned to hide

Joanne Ross

Soldier Boy

Oh soldier boy keep on walking
Drive out those terrorists that's stalking
You fight for freedom, and the right
To make your country safe and tight
To oust out evil to make purity
To reassure the insecurity
At what price your life will pay?
I wouldn't want you to, I pray
You and others, we hope God is by your side
We know you carry fear in your hearts, but feelings you have to hide
It's not a matter of national pride
Saving face I can confide
Being proud and standing tall
Fighting hard and fighting for all
For what you fight for is, right
You, and others with all your might
America and our United Kingdom could never fall
One unity, one people, one call
For stars and stripes, and the red, white and blue
The ensign for freedom for all of you
What price will you have to pay?
For others, I cannot say

Terry Powell

The Vain Stag

One day in the mountains beside a clear pool
A handsome young stag who had just finished school
Caught his reflection held fast in the water
And gazed at himself and vowed that he'd alter
The spindly legs he was born with and then
Admired his beautiful antlers just when
He heard the faint baying of wolves in the air
And so startled leapt in the woods where a snare
Of overwrought branches grasped at his crown
And snapped at his antlers and held him fast down
And closer and closer the snarling wolves raced
And try as he might he just couldn't unlace
The *fingerettes* curling themselves round his head
Resigning himself to becoming *quite* dead
And food for the wolves who were nearly upon him
He silently said both a prayer and a poem
When just at that moment by ceasing his struggle
The branches were loosened from their *jumble-juggle*
And freed from his captors he bounced down the lane
Away from the wolves 'til he reached once again
The pool in the mountains, so silent, so calm
So free from the fears and the chase and the harm
And gazing down where only small fishes swam
He said to himself, 'How lucky I am!
My beautiful antlers near brought me to death
While my ugly, stick legs mean I still have the breath
Of life living through me,' and musing on that
The handsome young stag on his way home from school
Took a shiver-deep sip from the icy, clear pool.

Goblet Boodles

Joy!

I love watching your happiness!
I don't drink, I only thirst on your tears of joy!
I laugh at your happiness
I am your first birthday
I am a bright rainbow
I survive on your laughter
I am Joy!

Poppy Harding (13)

Far ... Far Away

The day was quite lazy ... humidity high ...
No sign of a cloud in a rich, azure sky.
I leaned on my thoughts ... I was far, far away ...
There was little might make this a more perfect day.

I uttered, 'Dear Lord ... You bless me so much ...
I'm so glad we're true friends ... that You're not just a crutch ...
To make up for my frailties ... You are so much more ...
No wonder I seek You to love and adore.'

The Lord was yet silent ... but I knew He was there ...
His heart ever open ... receiving each prayer.
It's in His time He answers ... as I wait on Him ...
Enhancing life's purpose ... laying down each worldly whim.

In God's beautiful garden ... that's where He placed me ...
With Jesus my Saviour ... for all eternity.
What more could one ask than His perfect peace ... ?
The friend who died for me ... to gain my release.

The day was yet perfect ... through God's discerning eye ...
Still no sign of a cloud in the deep azure sky.
Only He could have made it a more perfect day ...
I went back to my thoughts and drifted far ... far away.

Kent Brooksbank

Armistice

The dying leaves of autumn drift across a tangled wooded scene.
The shrill cries of the birds are heard above the burnished paths beneath.
How deep the grief, how great the cause for fallen enemy and foe
For war bites deep into our hearts and takes no prisoners when we weep.
Campaigns are fought and won and lost, and in the seasons of our lives
And in the history of our age, we are the guardians of the past.
And like our fellow man before, we harbour every human vice
That tears the nation states apart in grief and human sacrifice.
But then the new dawn breaks once more and new recruits take up the call
And one by one I see again
A thousand fluttering poppies fall.

Margaret Whitehead

The Light And The Eye

The light entered the eye and spoke:
'What shall I show you today?
I have come a long way -
It's a million billion gigarillion wave-lengths from the sun!
I've glanced off a crescent moon -
Glittered on a blue lagoon -
Refracted through a rainbow -
What do you want to know?
I am the glory of the world, am I not?
You, little eye-dot,
That can scarcely move from the spot -
Where would you be without me?'

The eye blinked, and replied:
'Were I not here to see,
What joy would your glory be?
Who then would tell your tale of cosmic travels through light-years?
No soul would be aware
Of how your sunset colours flare.
No one would ever even know
There existed a rainbow!
Without me, you, Sun's radiant daughter,
Would dance to barren blindness on the water!
You, brilliant, bodyless,
Touchless, limitless -
Where would you be without me?'

Helgi Öpik

Anthology In Search Of A Title

Written in blood, centuries before,
passing for a treatise on peace,
an anthology on the Poetry of War

Where warmongers strut cocksure,
find hope's desperate pleas,
written in blood, centuries before

Eyes on glory at victory's glass door,
politicians deliver fine speeches,
an anthology on the Poetry of War

Pride spilling over on the home shore
for defeating its enemies,
written in blood, centuries before

Love, waiting in the wings evermore
can but weep at brave eulogies,
an anthology on the Poetry of War

Generations marking its pages as sure
as next autumn's leaves;
an anthology on the Poetry of War,
written in blood, centuries before

Roger N Taber

Soldier, Soldier

Deep in the burning desert sands
Death walks in the shadows of our children
Who donned their countries' cloth and armour
The bullet that is death travels on the wind
Invisible, unseeing, blind, silent
A thumping, tearing carnivore

Another soldier died today
I know because the newsman said
And no one stopped to grieve or say
Not knowing he had gone . . . was dead
Now lying in a cold deep grave

Oh men of my country who died like cattle
Who prayed to God as machine guns rattled?
. . . Mown down in your youth you asked for so little
A single drum beats slow, beats slow
Death is silent, fully loaded, encased in steel
Know it is death, it is death incarnate

Young men marched by rank on rank
Old soldiers watched along the flanks
But the soldiers who had the choice of God
And are mortal once again
Can never sleep upon gentle clouds
Of innocence again

Did society know them then?
When shed of their cloth and armour
They walked unknown, unsung, unseen
Knowing the freedom they had won
Yet their dreams are death's dark shadow
Their tears are lost in dry salt lakes
Strangers they stand, stark silhouettes
Smile a little longer than you or I
. . . Staring at the setting sun

UNITED IN INSPIRATION - The Golden Grove Appeal Poetry Collection

Young widows dressed in darkest night
Black tulips in the breaking dawn
With dewdrop tears upon their cheeks
Stand alone forlorn
Mothers' tears run like rivers
Who wore the reaper's shroud?
What glory ever came from war?
Silent the fatherless children held by the hand
Time will pass, time will heal the broken heart
The hand on the clock is turning fast
Soon peace will seal the scabbard to the sword

Row upon row of white headstones
Snake up rolling hills to distant horizons
The sun casts sharp shadows
Turns the ground to a symmetrical mosaic
Each piece a moment's horror of war
And tears like rain fall on the world
That wash the white headstones

A grandmother's hair, silver stolen from the moon
Her eyes bright as the stars of Orion
Sat in the church in solitary vigil
Myriads of colours
Filtered through the stained glass windows
The sun fell upon the altar
And the cross blazed in golden glory
As autumn leaves shifted and swirled
A dog howled from a distant farm
She arose slowly
Walked back to her grandchildren's laughter and song

Do not forget the price of freedom
After the sun has set, remember
Remember wrapped in midnight's blackness
For the night is full of sadness

And all the people said Amen.

David M Walford

Life Goes On

'Life goes on', so they say,
But my friend . . . passed away.
My life was shattered, it came to an end,
I lost my flatmate, playmate and a best friend.
The world went on without a care,
This didn't seem right, it wasn't fair.
Everything in my world stopped as if in a dream,
With an empty sinking feeling so it seemed.
I'd wake up and find he had gone,
I didn't have the chance to say, 'So long.'
All the guilty and angry feelings then rushed in,
If only, if things were different and what might have been.
The question - why did it happen? springs to mind,
This is an answer you may never find.
Don't dwell on what happened, you must move on,
This is big step, to smile and carry on.
Think of the special times that you did share,
A chat, a laugh, and not a care.
The nights out and a takeaway indoors,
The memories you had behind closed doors.
Remember . . . in this way,
As those memories won't fade away.
Precious, unique moments for only you to remember,
Watching, participating and discussing rugby and agriculture.
Live each day as if it's your last,
Life is a challenge from the very start.
The lessons of life are a tough test,
We are here to learn and do our best.
To appreciate what we have, to learn and grow,
So, now is the time to let go.
And memories will live on,
And as they say, 'Life goes on'.

Bethan Walters

Looking Back

Satisfied,
I hope you're satisfied
that you've taken my life
and turned it upside down.

No regret,
I know you have no regret
for the torture you put me through
and the hours I cried over you.

So much pain,
I went through so much pain,
I just wanted you to like me
and accept me for who I am.

Happiness,
that's what I'm feeling now,
true happiness
and I'm creating a brand new me.

Jane Vickers

Tell Me

Tell me, how would you face an imminent death?
Tell me, could you face the inevitable truth?
Wake every morning knowing it could be your last
And not sink under with doom and gloom.
The courage it takes is bound to our faith.
I am telling you,
Do not ask the question or demand any proof.

Linda Hearne

The Weeping Willow
(Written in honour of my oldest friend, Emma Naylor)

Remember the weeping willow?
It used to be our playground
A place to run and hide
And watch the world go by
It was the best weeping willow
A place we couldn't be found
We'd play side by side
And watch the world go by

Great friendships last forever
I believe we have that bond
I miss being together
It used to be so much fun
Remember skating in the park
And eating chips in the dark
Used to be so much fun

Then I went and moved away
But you were still my best friend
And you still are to this day
As great friendships have no end
Remember letters in the post
Sent to me on the coast
Great friendships have no end

Years went by, we stayed in touch
Excited with our lively news
Though we didn't write that much
It was as if I'd never left
Remember photos on email
Of our childhood trail
It was as if I'd never left

Suzy Turner

The Battlefields Of Love

With ego deflated and injured pride,
a heart that's now broken, and more beside.
From Cupid's sharp dart he's a victim of.
Lost his fight on the battlefield of love.

He read the poster, it told nothing new,
'The army will make a man out of you'.
Ireland, the Falklands, then Afghanistan,
you leave as a boy, return as a man.

Ego now boosted and bursting with pride.
Brave on the surface, but deep down inside
a voice warns, 'You could be the target of
stray bullets on this battlefield you love.'

Land mines exploding, all Hell is let loose.
Men blown to pieces. He thinks, *what the deuce
is this bloody war all about?* But then
explosion! Chaos! He whispers, 'Amen.'

With ego now crushed, and minus a limb,
hobbling on crutches his future looks dim.
Painful and clumsy his every move,
he now dreads life's real battlefield of love.

Stump bandaged and tender, early days yet,
but at least he's alive, no cause to fret.
He remembers his mates, brave to the last,
a hero soldier boy, killed in the blast.

With ego thus boosted, and head held high,
he grins at his chums, says his last goodbyes.
He jokes, saying one thing he's certain of -
part of him's on the battlefield he loved.

Mike Silkstone

Home For Heroes

To those who come to this bright land,
We'll gather close to hold your hand,
Knowing things have been rough for you,
Bodies to mend - your dreams to come true.

We know you are needing that special caring,
Both minds and bodies, for swift repairing.
Come to a beautiful country setting,
Healing and loving hands you'll be getting.

With Welsh fresh air, a country park -
A wonderful house to relight the spark
So many of you need right now -
To get you well will be their vow.

Soon, back home, all mended and strong,
But you'll be glad you came along.
Whatever your journey, wherever you go,
You'll feel much better, and not be low.

Heather E Cook

We Need Each Other!

'Your country needs you,' Kitchener said then,
Then off to war went our brave men,
Many of them paid the ultimate price
And laid down their lives in sacrifice,
Then the U-boats were sent to threaten our plight,
Up to the mark stepped our forces to fight.
Now they keep the peace in the Middle East,
Trying to tame the big terrorism beast,
They risk their lives to keep the peace in tact,
While always acting with integrity and tact.
'Your country needs you,' is what Kitchener said,
But sometimes our forces need our help instead.
Our forces are known worldwide as the best,
Having served many years being put to the test,
Respect our heroes for the job they have done,
Sometimes their own battles can never be won.
We must remember when our forces aren't well
And help them through their own personal hell.

Gary Maeslan

Absence Makes The Heart Grow Fonder

We've been away now for over six weeks
But we're not quite sure what our employer seeks
The morale was high and the intentions keen
Though knowledge of our future was not foreseen.

Although we are doing our everyday chores
And occasionally visiting Italian shores
We would much rather be at home with our kin
Because interest and tempers are getting quite thin.

We've started to plan for a 'Sod's Opera' type show
And most of the troops are having a go
The Army will act and the Navy will sing
To break the boredom, we'll try anything.

The lads below in the 150 man mess
Are living in conditions of very high stress
They are trying their hardest in learning to cope
It's really surprising they have not given up hope!

When we get our mail we are really glad
But it's not very often which is very sad
As we need our letters to keep in touch
With our family and friends who we miss so much.

So we live each day with a hope in our hearts
That we'll soon be leaving these dismal parts
And setting sail for the UK shore
To be at home with our loved ones once more.

Jim Kimpton

Friend

A flower may die,
The sun may set,
But a friend like you,
I'll never forget! Your name is precious!
It will never grow old! It's engraved in my heart!
In letters of *gold!*

Safia Siddique (14)

Born Free

All neatly tied up with some string,
How sad an ending, this poor thing.
Once strutted proudly, free as air,
It scratched and pecked without a care.
Blue sky above, green grass around,
A better place could not be found.
It thrived, it grew and put on weight,
Not knowing what would be its fate;
Across the road in battery shed,
Poor chickens might as well be dead.
Crammed together by the score,
Quite well fed but nothing more.
No air, no light, no room to fly,
Makes a free range chicken cry.
But unbeknown to this sweet bird,
No radio so it's never heard,
The end for both is still the same,
They have to die, oh such a shame.
Their lifestyle makes no difference now,
Before the butcher both must bow.
Then why do I waste precious time,
Writing you this little rhyme?
It's all about the quality,
The free range chick is best you see.
Aroma, taste and tender meat,
Mouth-watering and very sweet.
Convinced? There's nothing more to say,
I'll rest my case and go away.

Iago AP Llewellyn

The Flowers Of Never Ever

Behold the Temple of the Dawn
where the glow of Life is born
in multitude
the world's prelude
blossoms forth and spreads
across the sleepers' beds
in a golden glowing mine
it comes, a good new time
nudges open sparkling eyes
to see things of small size

wait on the brink my friends
all the worlds find their ends
but there is a place to find
through a rabbit hole in your mind
that leads to the open space
with room in which to amaze
a place that will live forever young and strong
with no space for things that are wrong
follow me
or let be

make room there ye mighty
I will become more than slightly

let me take you to the heart
where all creation did start
like a place lost in the old shifting sand
but, never caught in the destruction of Wonderland
lies the spirit of Eden
and the Flowers of Never Ever

Felix Erasmus

Mother And Son

'Mum, I'm joining the Army,'
Serious look upon his face
'I just have to do something
To get out of this rat race.'
I look at him with horror
My boy is just a lad
What has happened to his hopes and dreams
To be a toolmaker, like his dad?

I tell him I'll support him
Whatever he'll choose to be
After initial shock, I feel quite proud
He's joining the military
He puts the wheels in motion
Starts Army prep course straightaway
He returns, a student at college
Doesn't even miss a day!

Next comes the Army training
My boy is starting to change
He stresses over ironing
A4 folding, before putting away!
He passes out, not long later
A day I'll always remember
The fitness, marching, award ceremony
Means so much to his proud family

Then I get the dreaded call
'Mum, we're off to Afghanistan.'
I take awhile to take this in
My boy's not yet a man
I learn a lot about blueys
And send parcels via Royal Mail
The news all looks so different now
Got to watch it every day

The months go by so slowly
But he phones me up sometimes
The chat is always basic
The enemy may be listening on the lines
His welcome home party is sorted
Can't wait to see my lad
Big signs are made by his sister
When he's home, we'll be so glad

The party is a big success
He stands out proud from all the rest
His family, friends, people he doesn't know
Shake his hand until it is time to go
My boy came back a man from Afghanistan
But a change is taking place
Can't put my finger on it
But I can tell it in his face

He goes out a lot to have a drink
Always a joker with his friends
But he is doing this to blank the demons
That are constantly on his mind
'Mum, I want to leave the Army
Can't take it any more
Want to get out of that rat race
Or it'll be the death of me.'

I start to do some research
I have heard of PTSD
Post Traumatic Stress Disorder
Is there anyone who can help me?
Yes, there is a lot of help out there
Groups of people, just like me
They have had the training
In and out of the military

Jeanette Hopkins

The Golden Dream
(Dedicated to my son Craig - love you babe)

What would I do, what would I say, if I met the folks of yesterday?
I'd love to meet my cousins too, and grandparents I never knew.
Would they tell me life was good, or they survived on little food?
Did winter fires blaze so bright, or did they shiver through the night?
When man and boy went off to war, did families just struggle more?
Did they chase their aspirations, or simply follow their relations?
Butcher, Miner, Fire-fighter, Watchmaker or Street lighter?
Did they dress in hand-me-downs or best-of-fashion frilly gowns?
Did they wear shoes that made them tall, or sadly, have no shoes at all?
When they were sick, what did they do? Would doctors call to see them through?
So many things I want to know, if only they could tell me so.
Then I would tell them what *I* see in the 21st century.
Huge TVs hang on the wall. From anywhere we make a call.
Computers, printers, Xbox games, fashion clothes from *the* top names.
We tan our skins, wear nails of plastic, reshape our bodies to look fantastic.
Several holidays abroad will stop the kids from getting bored.
Fast food diners mean 'no cooking'. Who needs exercise like walking?
We have it good from what *they* knew. But sadly, there's a dark side too.
While we enjoy our modern toys, our rainforests are destroyed.
Exotic animals and creatures used for money-making ventures.
Devastated habitats no longer there for apes and cats.
They are shot, no care at all, so they can hang on someone's wall,
Or caged in squalor to comply to Man's demands, until they die.
Creatures border mass extinction while Man pursues his own perfection.
Our seas, unsafe from devastation and oil-polluted persecution.
Fins removed from living fish so Man can buy a 'tasty dish'.
Mass killing of the whale and shark will eventually leave its mark.
When creatures cannot reproduce, what will happen to the rest of us?
And even space beyond our skies is vulnerable to enterprise.
With space junk floating in the air, no one knows what could occur.
Monsoons and floods now set the pace while climate change is commonplace.
There is so much I want to say but sadness now gets in the way.
I want to tell my family that I'm ashamed of what I see.
And would the folk of yesteryears feel my disgust and share my fears?
Would they, like me, say, 'That's enough, let's stop this madness. Let's get tough.
Let's change our attitude to life. Let's stop the anarchy and strife.
Let's work together as a team. We *can* achieve our golden dream.
Let's stop the slaughter. Make a stance. Give animals a fighting chance.
Let's protect and utilise, and get the world to supervise.
Persuade all nations to take part. The time is now when we must start.
Tomorrow is too far away. Our creatures must be saved today.'

If I could meet my relatives, we could discuss the positives.
Would we agree on steps to take? Or ways to stop the heartbreak?
Would we think like one another and feel that change *is* worth the bother?
I'd love to meet my family, the old folks that have moulded me.

Sylvia Hughes

Another's Son, Another's Daughter
(Dedicated to those who work in areas of conflict to provide relief to those in need)

Another's son, another's daughter,
Today they live and work amongst gunfire and matters

To undertake a task that many others would not accept,
To assist other nations and their peoples protect.

To heal those who are injured, to safeguard their homes,
So they may live, work and in their homeland freely roam

Not persecuted for their birth, creed, religion or race,
Not forced to seek refuge in another far off place

So in time their precious mountains and fertile farmlands
Will be governed by virtuous and democratic hands

So in time the text written in the archived history books
Is that other nations did not stand by and just merely look.

Lieutenant Commander Lorraine England
Queen Alexandra's Royal Naval Nursing Service

Love Letters

Joy writing sparklers
circle and whip against
blistering roast chestnut bonfire heat.

She knows it is time to say goodbye
bluebird letters tied with red
a combustible time bomb of gangrenous spores.

It seems a pity

they had sustained
through enforced absence
sizzling in a secret drawer
and seeing again
wads of spidery writing
shoe horned into fingered envelopes
she regretted the action that had to be taken

cremation.

So she force fed the flames
as the guy crumbled
and golden rain fell from a gloved hand.

Jill Govier

A Call To Sing

My desire is to sing
for the courts of Heaven to ring
in sweet melody to the King
like the flap of an angelic wing.

I will sing to Him with my voice
and in His presence rejoice
His beautiful throne I will raise
by a great song of praise
with His given grace
in every place.

I will sing about His endless glory
and daily about The Calvary Story
I will sing about His Word
and from Him what I have heard.

I want to be in The City where there is great peace and calm
and joyfully sing my psalm
and also sing my hymn
nicely and only to Him.

Michael Kwadwo Poku

One Night In Tiree

Out of the sky-blue
bus we flocked,
where eagles soared
and corncrakes mocked,
where white sands fled
the broken hour glass,
a bold, flirtatious sea
frilled into ribbons
of blue and ultra marine,
surf caressed Balephuil's
glistening crescent clean,
clover scented machair
cushioned each footfall so,
when we looked back
we could not even see
the place where we had been.

As if waking from a dream,
we queued on the jetty
and watched The Clansman seem
to grow out of the glassy sea.
While we still clung to memory,
mobiles began to chirp,
searching for a signal,
searching for another world,
round the clock coverage,
the death of a superstar,
a media monster rising
unbidden from the deep.

With such tentacles reaching everywhere,
who could blame the ones who could not see
what we still see, nor understand our yearning
for just one more night on Tiree.

Richard Jones

Cricket On The Green
(Dedicated to all those who served in the Great War)

Old pals standing side by side,
In the summer sun shining bright,
Cricket on the green their final sight
As our boys go off to fight.

Ypres and Somme and Paschendale,
Through all the wars' living Hell,
Loved ones wait back at home,
Nights in trenches chill soldiers' bones.

Four years pass,
Boys to men grown so fast,
Returning back to England's shores at last,
Back to homes' green grass.

A memorial stands to them,
To every boy and every man,
Veterans gather, those who can,
To lay poppies on the green.

S R Hurley

Time
(In memory of our son Matthew,
who came down in his plane at the age of 30)

Only through time, time is conquered
Time is a healer - I think not
Pain eats away and hits at the spot
Each moment restored, each memory shot
Only through time, time is conquered
Positive thoughts produce no gain
When guilt overtakes and magnifies shame
Only through time, time is conquered.

Gael Nash

War Memorial!

It stands conclusively, beyond doubt
As a proud monument that follows
The shadow. The minion font neither
Nonpareil nor brevier holds its own
To have that entry and like a breath
Expressing slowly it does not prove
Except where stone has met the chisel.
It is amongst the silent letters
As witness to a perfect crime - long
Added as a chapter to the world -
The glorious dead with that epitaph
Dissembling, not held within this fold
Yet found a home in perpetuity
As if inscribed by timeless thought.

William Birtwistle

To Andy

On a dark and frosty night
when the stars are shining bright
'tis then the spirits come to call
and the tears begin to fall.
If you would be so bold
as to stand out in the cold
who knows what you'd see?
You might, yet, see me.
Gone now to eternal rest,
no more around to joke and jest.
In your memory I'll last,
an echo from the past.

Anne Anderson

A Little Town

There is a little town I know
That means a lot to me
Its streets are not paved with gold
It's a long way from the sea

It was there in my grandfather's arms
As he celebrated the war end
It was there I went to school
It was there I made my first friend

It was there my father enjoyed a pint
My mother her glass of stout
It was there they had fish and chips
To end their Saturday night out

It is there I visit not and then
And sometimes shed a tear
Because of all the places I have lived
My heart still lives there

Patricia Stone

Gertrude's Wish

There was a little cow, Gertrude was her name
she wasn't like the other cows, her thoughts were not the same
she longed to be a horse as black as black could be
grazing in a field, roaming round so free
that's all she ever thought of, she was rather strange
hoping for the time that someday she would change
then one starry night she saw a wishing star
then she made a wish on the star so far
she woke up in the morning and into a horse she grew
Gertrude she was happy, her wish it had come true

J M Crook

Holding Hands
(In memory of Arthur Foster 1923-2010.
He fought in the Second World War for his country)

There is a garden where roses grow
forever blooming 'neath a summer sky
a place where loved ones gather close
and golden winged memories flutter by.

A healing garden bathed in light
where mortal ills can be undone
then sprinkled out across the ground
to melt like snowflakes, in the sun.

A sentient garden, calm and bold
where all your mortal fear is shed
and spiritual beauty clothed in love
will soothe your weary soul instead.

A garden given in perpetuity
where summer never ends
and we'll walk together there
for eternity, as friends.

Christine Williams

Depression

I live in the deepest, darkest corners of everyone's hearts.
I am a dark, shadowy corner, haunting you.
Black belongs to me,
I am the nightmare you can't escape.
Death is my only friend.
I don't eat food, but I steal your soul.
I thrive on loss and sadness.
I am every teardrop.
I am depression.

Rosie Plimmer (13)

The Old Man Of Gelli Aur

The daisies and the buttercups
the rhododendron blooms
lie scattered, fading, rotting
as soon the mansion looms.

A burst of light
a snapping twig
it all sounds so familiar
a whiff of smoke
a sudden shower
and then we see the warrior.

He sits alone
and looks across
to broken walls and windows
but far beyond
he can recall
the woods and mountain meadows.

He lifts his head
we gasp aloud
his wounds have barely healed
he says, 'Sit down -
this is the place
our future must be sealed.'

We talk awhile -
it's difficult
his voice grows soft and gruffer
he says his mates
have left him here
they've gone to see their maker.

'Us ones who're left will benefit
from such a fine location
A sanctuary
and helping hands
away from all that action.'

We turn to go
he says, 'Farewell,'
another flash of light
a whiff of smoke
the mansion fades
and he is out of sight.

Irene Hall

Alone In The Dark

Sun shines
Barefoot in the park
As I lie dreaming
Alone in the dark

You come to me
How I wish that you knew
The sun in the dark
It is just us two

Your smiling face
Does quicken my heart
Wonder where in my life
Will you play your part

The heart on my sleeve
I desperately hide
Sense the same is in you
As a matter of pride

Oh how we play
Two kids in that park
As I lie dreaming
Alone in the dark

Carla Stokes

Close To Heaven

All was silent as he felt
The softness of the grass
Beneath his skin,
Cupping his head in his hands,
He gazed at the clear
Blue of the sky,
A few white clouds drifted about,
Like huge balls of cotton wool,
He could hear the sigh
As all lived and breathed around him,
The warmth of the sun
Caressed and surrounded him,
With a wonderful sense of calm
Hugging his tortured soul
Closing his eyes he drifted
Off into a dreamless sleep,
Where no ghosts could haunt him,
All memories were in the distant past,
Their horrors wouldn't harm him,
This he felt was Heaven,
He was safe here at last.

Pauline Uprichard

On Top Of The Rhigos Mountain

Now my sweetie is Canadian
From the rocky mountains grand
And he tells me of the splendour
Of his wild and lovely land

So I thought, *well we have mountains*
Though his are topped with snow
Ours are still quite lovely
So up the hills we'll go

We set off very early
Taking coffee in a flask
To linger on the mountain
In Heaven's presence bask

Up and up we drove
Through country stark and grand
I thought, *there this will impress him*
Wales - the promised land

In splendid isolation
In accordance with my plan
We parked on top of the Rhigos
By 15 cars and the ice cream van

We drank in the view and the coffee
We held hands, my sweetie and me
And then I had a dilemma
As I really needed to wee

No trees on top of the Rhigos
Not a bush that was large and thick
It's OK and discreet to pee like a man
But a woman? We don't have a . . . hope in Hell of being as discreet

Anton said, 'No one will know you
No one will tell any tales.'
I said, 'Probably so true of Canada
But we're from a small town in Wales

Each person knows everyone's business
Six friends and two neighbours will pass
And I will be spotted and rumbled
At the moment that I bare my a***.'

Well girls - you all will know,
The more you talk about it, the more you need to go!

We talked of the problem together
For together we can face any odds
And I decided to crouch in the heather
And I sent up a plea to the gods

'Please God don't let anyone see me
Please God don't let neighbours drive past'
My back teeth were floating for ages
There was no way that I could be fast

The relief when it came was tremendous
Why did I get in such a stew?
The problem was braved and my dignity saved
We went back to admiring the view

We went home to the pub for a quick one
With the locals, a big merry band
A neighbour came in for a drink
With a wink says, 'The view on the Rhigos is grand.'

On and on went the greetings
Some kindly and others quite crass
But I sure had enough when the bartender said
'Lady, you've got one fine looking . . . jeep!'

When we win the lottery millions
A big house is not what I crave
I'll build a ty bach on the Rhigos
So women don't have to be brave.

Kathryn Wilkins

Happiness

I live in the warmth of your heart
I get rid of sadness
I make fun and laughter
I am a dream come true
A child's smile on Christmas Day
I am every happy teardrop
I am everybody's friend
I hate terrible words
I am happiness.

Sali Jones (13)

Golden Grove Haven

A grove of gold laburnum,
Full flower glory in the sun;
Pictured, dancing memories
Wafting through sunlit times.

The Service person stands.

Boiling hate brings fear; crouched
Youth and age, tremble surrounded.
By deep ire, greed, force impounded:
A terrible destiny; prayer expanded.

The Service person fights, falls.
The Service person stands.

Protected people relax, well defended;
Memory of terror, anguish, pain has faded.
Democracy gleams but price appended;
Service children, parents mourn dejected.

The Service person fights, dies,
The Service person fights, ails,
The Service person stands.

People rescued, saved, freed;
People in remembrance stand.
We recognize with pride, sacrifice,
We see, awed; no payment suffice.

Daphne G Davies

Ambition

I live in the mind
I give people confidence
I take knocks and falls
but make people carry on
I'm what people dream about
yet I make them get up in the morning
I strive to be the best
The best need me to succeed
I am ambition.

Victoria Moulson (13)

Tomorrow

Tomorrow I will drink in the morning dew as I watch the sun rise,
For it's home I've come, away from distant lands,
Where the battle for change is a long drawn out charade.
I shall listen to the raindrops as they sing a different tune,
And wonder at the glory of it, in my land I call my own.
I have missed the simpler things in life like the heralds of the dawn, the rustle of the leaves as the wind blows through
And the trickling of the brook which whistles past my home.
I have yet to watch a dragonfly struggling from its cocoon,
But I feel its suffering now as my fight begins,
Trying to unravel the tragedy as it unfolds within my brain.
And I'm glad to see the rolling hills, the valleys and the dales,
To hear my fellow dialect not words I can't comprehend.
My mother how I've watched as she's tried to hide her pain,
to see her once perfect son now has missing limbs,
But she smiles on bravely, at least she has her son,
Whilst others less fortunate can only tend their sons' or daughters' graves.
Tomorrow I will drink in the morning dew,
Utter a silent prayer, for when I thought I'd taken my final breath it was home I dreamt about.

Jane Margaret Isaac

Without You

Without you, life's not complete,
I search for you in empty streets.
Shuttered doorways, windows barred,
Without you, my life's so hard.

Without you to take my hand,
Hopes I had, now castles of sand.
Self-awareness all shot to hell;
Sealed in by destiny, Fate's tolling bell!

Without you to guide my ways,
To give me purpose every day,
You! The first to make me see;
To be with you is to be free.

Without you, all I can say,
I hope, and wish, to find a way.
To make you truly understand, that,
Without you, I'm only half the man.

Raven Pal

Confusion

I am all question marks,
I live in your mind.
I'm every maths test,
I am as old as you.
I'm a lost child in a theme park,
I look like a spiral.
I make you puzzled,
I eat what you understand.
I'm a blind man that can see
And a deaf man that can hear.
I'm a fish trapped in a glass tank,
When I am at my best you are at your worst.

Elin Hopkins (13)

Fear

I am black and unknowing,
I am like the night,
I thrive on every scream, every wince,
I am the thing that goes bump in the night,
I lurk in dark alleys,
I live on the irrational part of your mind,
I inspire scary movies,
I am the voice in the back of your head telling you to turn around,
I spend my time drinking tears,
The Grim Reaper is my closest friend,
I am *fear!*

Kate Jasperse (13)

Fireworks

I wrapped up warm in my scarf and hat,
The sky was dark and clear, but wait, what was that?
I set out walking at a brisk pace,
And I thought I saw something in outer space.

I stopped to stare at the sight before me,
The sky was suddenly lit, but what could it be?
Sparks and bangs, shouts and cries,
An explosion of colour before my very eyes!

I approached a bonfire, warm and bright,
Flames, orange and yellow, oh what a sight!
What night is this? I must remember,
Of course, of course, it's the 5th of November!

Rosie Plimmer (13)

Hate!

I live in a dark black coffin
I was born on Friday 13th
I love funerals because I hate people
Halloween is the best time of year
I don't eat but I like eating people's souls
When people cry it makes me laugh
Grim Reaper is my best friend
I hate everyone and everything
I like it when people hate me
Teardrops are my life
I am horrific hate!

Sinead Murphy (13)

Bittersweet

I'm a cold-hearted killer,
Merciless in my ways.
I make you feel so anxious,
People crumble from my gaze.

Everybody wants me,
But will they when they find
The chaos and destruction
And the tears I leave behind?

It'll start off so happy,
But always end up sad,
Lying, cheating and hiding,
Humans can't help but be bad.

I hear you ask my name
Though I am such a powerful force.
Now you know the answer -
It's love, of course.

Adam Reaney (14)

Love

I am the tasty chocolate that melts in your mouth,
I live within your heart,
I make you happy,
I am your most lovable friend,
I buy you gifts at Christmas,
I am Valentine's Day,
I am your dreams.

Ffion Caines (13)

War Without End

Throughout our history there has been strife,
A cull of youth, through unremitting wars,
Struck down still in the very prime of life,
Through leadership, bereft of all remorse.
Humanity is such, there's always greed
For power, wealth, resources some have got,
But you have not, yet crucial is your need,
So you *must* have it all, or share the pot!
Now think of *other* leaders, who, in fear,
Defend themselves against the stronger might
Of superpowers resolved to domineer,
Regardless of whoever's in the right!
Add *dogma* and *belief*, which never cease,
To know the world will *never* be at peace.

Christopher Head

Fear!

I live in dark eyes
I make people scared
I am scared of smiles
I love making people run
I don't drink pop, but drink scared sweat
I only eat scared feelings
I am centuries old
I am fear!

Ryan Jones (13)

Death

Your last breath is my music,
A funeral is a job done well.
I'm the world's best undertaker -
I have a schedule for everyone's death.

I can draw your breath
like Picasso draws a painting.
I organize the death
and control the murderer's mind.

I do deals with the Devil
and steal souls from Heaven.
Hell is my home
and your dead soul is my food.

I feel lonely all the time
because I kill everyone I touch.
My blood is poisonous,
my skin is too hot to touch.

I exhale chlorine gas,
my hair is a tangle of mambas.
I change from one mythical creature to the next.
I am De*ath*.

Tom Cooze (13)

Peace

I live in the heart
I make friendship
I'm what is and what isn't
I destroy war and war destroys me
Friendship is my best friend
I love to sleep
I am peace.

Mathew Jones (13)

Fireworks

Swirling, coloured fireballs,
Twisting through the air.

Children's screams fill the neighbourhood
As their fireworks explode in the sky.

Dogs are kept in as their barks shout out,
Above a pretty moonlit night.

The burning sight of a guy
Lit on a smoking fire.

Sparkling Roman candles next door,
In lots of different styles.

The tasty scent of sausages, potatoes and hot chocolate
Filled my nose.

All my friends gathered round
To roast Guy-shaped marshmallows.

When I heard the boom of the final firework
I knew it was time to go.

Joe Leslie (13)

Against The Elements

A raincloud lingers above us.
The rain beats down on our bodies but we carry on.
Thunder rattles in our heads, echoes in our hearts.
But we carry on.
The flash of lightning blinds us, but we do not cower, we do not stop.
And we will not stop until the sun begins to shine once again.

Sierra Gaffney

Our Armed Forces

It's when you give
All
Or nothing left in
For a new day

It's when you go at it
Strong
Something there
For tomorrow

Consider the lilies in the field
Or the sparrows in their nest
Our Armed Forces similar
Need a place to rest

But if weakness lies
Without our hearts
Strength is by our side
Our Armed Forces benefit

Concern, care or share
This world of ours
They who fight the good fight
Remain, sincerely, yours - The Poet!

S M Thompson

What If

Something awful has just happened,
And those words enter your head,
You think about them again and again,
As you lay silently in your bed,

In the morning they're still there,
Guilt is feeding off that phrase,
Thinking back into the past,
Considering different ways,

But it is impossible to change,
What has already been done,
But don't give up because you know,
That your guilt has not yet won,

Disintegrate those silly words,
Because they cannot help you heal,
Swallow all that useless guilt and,
Express how you really feel,

Two words can influence your thoughts,
Don't let them control your life,
Or let guilt control your emotions,
As you'll begin to live in strife,

'What if' is a silly phrase,
It cannot change the past,
So push it out of your mind,
And you'll be at peace at last.

Charlotte Beaumont-McAllen

Different Dreams

I believe in dreams . . .

Not the ones that belch out of my fatigued nerves
Neither those insinuated under vicarious spells of instant soporifics.

Time and again how uncontrollably I would be swayed
By them . . .
Into the incoherent puddle of shivering fantasy and tit-bits of subconscious realities,
A hazy hairline merger of acrid reality and life . . .
A tempting seduction between sacrilege and sanctimony
The ones that intertwine me into sublime shackles of trance
And drive me amidst gullies of shadowy slums and monolith paradises.
Amidst chivalrous ruins of lethal outbursts
Apathetic faces and venal hearts
Mocking fiascos and classical illusions
Amidst heinous nights and cognac afternoons

I hate to surrender before this nonchalant force
That so effortlessly drags me
Against the currents of heady nostalgia and amorphous remembrance
Ethnic passions and gargoyle realities
Clichéd folklores and electric rancor
Sanguinary cataclysms and eclipsed sunshine

I hate dreams that manipulate reality

My reality . . .

That taunt and tease the bearings of unaware siestas
That's me . . .
Dreamless adolescence swept me into adulthood
Unmoved by tantalising ripples of dreamy incense
Dormant subtleties suddenly brimming over scalding cauldrons
Yet the child still hides behind facades of sullen memories

(Memories:
A sky full of green gossamer parakeet wings
A pale pallet of amber conscience stretches as far as the benevolent dusk
Where gods glide in their airy avatars
Life clings to the paragon wings of tarnished falcons)

A square room, a square earth . . . a bottled existence
The all powerful genii that I had dreamt (in memories)

Reality:
The powerless soundless clamour of fragmented entities
Opaque smog of ennui that stifles the echoes
Hydra-headed lust that encompasses frantic breaths of freedom
And unholy divinity smothers the ambience breathless
Inarticulate babbling is all that is left
Of a once magniloquent sonnet of life
Thus I believe in life that like the potter's impeccable artistry
Chums porcelain dreams out of shapeless mounds
And I believe in dreams that promise me the unfathomable promise of life
I believe in dreams that mark the renaissance dawn breaks
The dreams of organza moonbeams
And dreams of hazy winter mornings
And earthly aroma of dews
Savant understanding, intellectual portrayals
That is life for me . . .

A cul-de-sac that ushers an unperturbed purple horizon
Those are my dreams . . . different dreams

Ritam Goswami

Tears Of Our Soldiers

The depths of our soldiers' saddened eyes
Tells a story which holds no lies
Pain and death which they bury so deep
Only their eyes betray them as they weep
Concealed so deep they try hard to forget
But pain grows within their young tender hearts
Only to surface in a solitary tear
Gently falling from their wounded face
The tears they cry descend to a pool of pain
Reliving the horrors of war again and again
Brave young soldiers, must you cry
For every past friend you dared watch die?
Solitude becomes your appropriate friend
Your own troubled souls, you're left to defend
Can we understand the world you must live?
Your body, your soul, you readily give
Fight on young soldiers, be brave, be bold
We will remember you all, young and old.

Wendy Shone

Life

Life is sunshine,
Life is rain.
Life is laughter,
Life is pain.
Life is colour,
Life is grey.
Life is night,
Life is day.
Life is hope,
Life is worry.
Life is peace,
Life is hurry.
Life is sorrow, anger, grief.
Life is love, joy, relief.

Rachel Sutcliffe

It's Heaven

In the ancient halls of Heaven
by the sparkling crystal sea
on the shore of Lake Forever
that's where my soul will be

In the fresh green grass of Eden
I shall pass my restful days
in the shade of the tree of life
I'll find where my love lays

In God's own son I'll cherish
all the love I miss on Earth
and in the garden of His presence
I shall find my life's rebirth

In the joy of Heaven's glory
I'll know myself secure
forever in the arms of love
my soul will be so pure.

Daphne Cornell

For The Shilling

They've been taking the shilling for many a year
And then they've been marching to war
And many a mother or wife shed a tear
For fear that they'd see them no more

Over centuries passed they have answered the call
To fight for the land that they loved
Some would come back again but so many would fall
And we asked just what was it they'd proved?

Well to ask it of them is the wrong thing to do
For they did what their duty demands
And the sacrifice given was for me and you
When they went to those forsaken lands

In the deserts and forests all over the world
In the mountains and over the plains
As the armies drew up and the banners unfurled
Soon discoloured by mankind's bloodstains

They are doing it now in a vast barren land
Duty calls and the hearts are still willing
Though their friends have been torn and have died in the sand
Still they hold out their hands for the shilling.

Castallaman

Paper Lake

A broken mirror waits in the rain
To open its heart to a window frame,
Then hidden reflections gather together
To scamper across the face of the mirror,
And huddle forlornly by the empty frame
As they wait in a queue for a cue to go in
(Lost for now, but sometimes seen again
Whenever the clouds crowd together
To spoil the view with more bad news).

Robert Black

The Maid Of Orleans

I can hear the hare in the grass,
The whisper of clouds across the sky,
And the militant singing of the saints.
All, all call me.

Their soft and sacred voices
Seep me in power and glory;
Their holy music
Makes mute the sounds of men.
My distant king strokes my heart,
I pierce the flesh of his enemy.

I do not inhabit my girl's narrow body
But roam, triumphant, with hare and cloud and the company of saints,
March to their sweet sounds and whispered chanting,
Their war chorus of wonder
Buoys me with valour,
Leads me to embrace the sword, the pike and the armour,
Follow the pounding hooves, the cries of the warriors.
All, all carry me to enthralling battle
For my king, God's Chosen One.

Lifted by the voices of the saints,
Float, fly, sing loud my battle song.
In my purity, I, a soldier
Fight, slash, stab, hoist high
My banner of victory,
Deliver my king to the sacrament of his crowning.

Then is the catastrophe.

I am forsaken
To silence. Silence.

Unheeded, helpless
Falling down,
Through invincible cosmic rifts,
Into a place
Beyond my understanding:
Blood sex laws men.

The coursing hare, the dreaming cloud, the singing saints
No longer calling, no longer calling me shining, brave and innocent.
Lonely, so lonely.

From tower, leap;
Heart stumbles in the grass,
Thins across the sky, bleeds red the leaves of the trees.

Afraid, so afraid.
Scorned as soldier, mocked as woman,
Cower at hard tones of common sense,
Cover ears
From the snarling scorn of priests,
The clanking of chains,
The bruising drone of justice
And whooping cries of cruelty.

Better, then,
The men take me
Strip me naked
Tie the stake
Burn me alive.
Better than hearing only
The noise of men.

Tessa Paul

It's You

It's you who breathed life into my lifeless life,
You who gave thoughts for my thoughtless mind,
And you who brought joy into my empty eyes.

You give me love for my loveless heart,
Strength for my arms, power to my frame,
And now I must thank you and just want to say,
'Come live inside me, and guide me today'.

David Sawyer

Reclaim The Nation

Arise ye patriotic clouds
And free the nation
From the images of the past
And speak the real greatness of the nation
Away from the superstitions of blood and ancestors
To the real place of those who made the nation their home
And built it stone by stone
Every day and all the day
As those who came from all the earth
Attracted by the prospect of a better life
And contributed their blood
Their sweat
Their tears
To the face of the nation reborn

And speak of the values of the past
The values of the present
And the future to come
A vision of the nation proud and free
Born again in knowledge of the past
Including all
In their times and their tears
Of the nation, one of people not of tribes
Nation of ideas and future
Not of superstitions and the past
To look forward not backwards
And include the many not the few
In that is greatness found
And the nation at ease with its past.

Alasdair Sclater

Beech Trees

Still grey and silent they stand
While I stir the leaves of last year's autumn
Pale sunlight threads their whispering branches
As I creep beneath their shade.

Strong with the strength of ages
Mute, in the nature of their ways,
No lips from which rank criticism falls,
Nor ears to hear, or eyes to see,
No limbs that flail, or blows to fall,
But sit upon their grasping, clinging roots,
That search among the fine pale stones.

So, leaning, feel the rugged trunk against my cheek
A sensuous, all pervading peace seeps through my being.
This steadfast stalwart, perhaps two centuries old,
Has watched the lover's tryst beneath its boughs
Has seen the shining river in the valley flow
While shepherds rended sheep upon the slope
Blackberries hanging, dewy ripe
While flushed young maidens baskets fill.
Then winter turns the flowing beck to storming swill,
Uprooting stones and tearing down the hill.

Now roads and houses clothe the lower slopes
And shining skeins of metal mark the railway lines.
High up the hill tall angled piles sling cabled power ropes,
A hum of distant traffic, drone of turbo jets,
With frozen aerial pistes high in the sky,
Muted ostinato below the theme and variation of the woodland slopes,
Clang of mechanic shovels and the thrum of radio sets.
Here in the haven of the trees, peace . . .

E Meletor Smith

Footprints In The Battlefield

One night as a soldier battled, for his life yes he fought
He could barely hear his own mind, its own single thought
Bullets flew like heavy rain, bombs exploded all around
His one thought his young wife, the love that he'd found

Their two young children too, nestled safely in her arm
Safe from madness he faced, out of reach, as to harm
Fearing his life's end nearing, he cried out bitterly to God
Battling through bombs and bullets, the fierce path he now trod

Envisioned God as a Father, clearly nestling him in His arm
Safe from madness around him, from any bullets or harm
He craved being with his family, rather than fighting this war
Then he heard someone call him, hopes built up once more

His colleagues shed a light, a way home out of this mess
As other soldiers died and fell added grief atop of his distress
Fearing for his children, his wife too, what life may bring
He, determined to battle on, regardless of Death's call and sting

Each and all of those soldiers, only now but a small few
Managed to get out in safety, to find their way through
Yet no colleagues were there, no one had shone the light
Battling for lives through that dark, bomb-strewn night

On returning next morning seeking any injured or dead
He could not understand, puzzled frown on his head
His path clearly defined, his own footsteps marked clear
Another had led his path right in front of him yet so near

He knew all full well, he'd fought this path, battling alone
Yet someone had led him, back to safety and to home
He clearly also reasoned from his path he should be dead
Each step he had took uncountable bullets had crossed or sped

Looking more closely, the other footprints showed bare feet
Someone had shielded him from bullets, death and defeat
Looking all around him, appearing amid a sun ray of light
Jesus, a myriad of angels, shining round him, glowing bright

Don't worry my child, I shielded you safely, from all harm
Guided each and every footstep, 'twas I took you by the arm
No moral here my child, no lesson, it's you called out to God
Call out often, any time, amid bullets in life's path you'll tread.

Christopher R Slater

Heal The Broken-Hearted
(Dedicated to all who mourn)

You kneel there all alone again and stare with empty gaze,
The pain of all you're going through is etched upon your face.
You struggle with the loneliness - it all seems so unfair,
But Jesus says, 'I love you, child, I want you in My care.'

Heal the broken-hearted! Heal the broken-hearted!

Why is it that you're so cast down and troubled in your soul?
Remember - always hope in God and He will make you whole;
Repair your sad and broken heart, for He can make it new.
Surrender now to His control - your spirit He'll renew.

Heal the broken-hearted! Heal the broken-hearted!

Let Jesus soothe your aching heart, the echo of your fears,
He'll hold you in His loving arms and wipe away your tears.
Just trust Him to take care of you, surrender to His will,
And He will guide you lovingly, your grieving spirit fill.

Heal the broken-hearted! Heal the broken-hearted!

He's promised you His endless care, for with Him you belong,
His loving kindness through the day, and in the night, His song.
Pray always to the God of life and He will hear your plea,
His everlasting arms will hold you through eternity.

Heal the broken-hearted! Heal the broken-hearted!

Jan Kerntiff

Soldier On

Over the lands and across the sea,
I know that you'll still be there for me.
But whilst you're away and in all that you do,
I want you to know I'll be thinking of you.
So take your courage, power, laughter and passion,
And fulfil your role aided by military ration!
You've amazing strength of mind, body and spirit,
So go live your dream, cherish every minute.

Ruth Tomkins

The Pumpkin People

Down in the pumpkin patch
Beneath the large green leaves,
The tiny people living there
Are working hard, their sleeves
Pushed up, they puff and pant
And dash from place to place.
They hang their lanterns overhead,
With extras, just in case
The glow worms in each foxglove
Forget to shine their light
And welcome guests might lose their way
In the darkness of the night.

The beetles act as waiters
They check out laden tables
While ladybirds in spotted coats
Inspect that all the labels
On the prizes are in place
As this is presentation time
When all contenders at the fete
Reciting rhyme, performing mime,
Flute playing, dragon snapping,
Shaking poppy seeds.
Rainbow painting, leaf blowing
Arranging flowers and weeds.
Tiny little fairy cakes and
Loaves of bread are spread,
Ready to be judged for taste
By the old, clan head.

The daylight fades, and one by one
The glow worms do their duty,
A soft green light spreads through the patch
The scene is one of beauty.
The largest pumpkin opens wide
And what a sight within!
The wide array of costumes
Of all the kith and kin
Who live in this mysterious place
Is met with huge applause.
The audience is seated
On the benches spread outdoors.

Beryl Henshaw

Incident In Baghdad

From Gary, Indiana,
and Duluth, from Baton Rouge
and Jackson, Mississippi,
from Butte, Montana
and from Birmingham they come,
six baby-faced GIs, red-eyed
from lack of sleep, six hardened,
three-month vets, crew-cuts beneath
their helmets' camouflage, shorn lambs,
like high school dropouts, truanting.

Hot in drab, military, olive-green
fatigues, alert, with rifles cocked,
watchful as foxes as they leave their den,
they shout, like conquerors, a warning,
then kick open the locked gates to storm
the compound. (Afterwards, back at base,
stretched out upon their cots, in letters
to their high school sweethearts,
they'll re-enact their mission, opting,
for once, for understatement, for litotes.)

They shout a warning, the conquistadors,
kick open the locked gates and storm
the compound. What hits them first's
the smell, the stench of s**t. And then
the baking heat, the desert sun streaming
through sealed, unshuttered, filthy glass.
There, on the concrete floor, like human slugs,
maggots with rickets, boss-eyed, with cataracts,
tiny cadavers, frail bird bones parchmented in sacs
of skin, twelve naked orphans spreadeagled in their filth.

One GI gags and heaves. The others weep.
Laying their rifles along iron springs,
they go from nightmare child to nightmare child.
Kneeling, they make a cradle of their arms.
Thin, stalk-like necks support the lolling heads,
the bone-sacs hold the flickering pulse of life.
Each soldier takes two corpses in his arms,
two weightless, small Pietás, oozing pain.
Bright, staring eyes that gazed into the abyss
gaze with rebuke and puzzlement again.

Norman Bissett

K-R-W

You are friendly, kind and caring
Sensitive, loyal and understanding
Humorous, fun, secure and true
Yes that's you.

Special, accepting, exciting and wise
Truthful and helpful, with honest ocean-blue eyes
Confiding, forgiving, cheerful and bright
Yes that's you.

You're one of a kind, different from others
Generous, charming, but most of all mine
Optimistic, thoughtful, happy and game
But not just another . . . in the long chain.

Appreciative, warm and precious like gold
Our relationship won't tarnish or ever grow old
You'll always be there, I know that is true
I'll always be here . . . always for you.

But if not for you I wouldn't know what true love really meant
I'd never feel this inner peace
Nor this happy and so content
If not for your tender touch
I'd miss the bliss of love's fun and craziness.
I have to hear your sweet voice daily
I know so much yet have so much more to learn
Nobody could ever take your place
One day in me you will believe and trust

Inside your arms is where I love to be
As the two of us become one
But so much distance is between us
I hope the miles won't one day come split us
But if not for you I'd be adrift
I'd be searching for my other half
Incomplete
If I hadn't ever met my soulmate
 . . . Yes, that's you.

Paulette Francesca Sedgwick

Epitaph For A Fallen Comrade

We found him in a foxhole,
Crawling in the mud.
His lower limbs blown apart,
His body caked in blood.

He screamed for us to end it,
Fractured features telling all.
No one disagreed with him,
But none would heed his call.

He seemed to moan forever,
A 'dead man' with a voice.
The volume of his pleading,
Casting doubt upon our choice.

Then darkness overcame him
And snatched him from his hell.
His final word was 'Mother',
Before an eerie silence fell.

Paul Kelly

Ode To An Oak Tree

If you could speak, or give some sign
From your experience,
How you would enlighten us
With all that you have seen.
Your majesty all shrouded in green beauty
Adorns our tedious world.
You eat our folly and give back life support
We little do deserve.
Food and shelter you freely giver to species numerous
With little thanks returned.
Time moves slowly in your world where only seasons count,
Opposed to our fanaticism.
Would that we could emulate your constancy
And humble sophistication.
Oh! wondrous oak relieve our tormented minds
From life's crassness,
So we may live once more in harmony with you
And no more search for inconsequence.

Norman Biggs

Of Dust

As the angry, burning, baleful sun
sets beneath the distant horizon,
its farewell leaving burnished plumes
of dust
hanging in the sky,
soldiers cast nervous glances
at ever-lengthening shadows.

With darkness encroaching
'pon sandbagged emplacements,
fingers tighten -
nervously -
on triggers.

Fists are formed, and unformed.

Sweat beads on eyebrows.

Eyeglasses are straightened
to keep out the swirling eddies of approaching storms
of dust.

Parties set out - not hens these,
but stags - sent to keep watch
o'er sleeping comrades.

As hour after incessant hour drags its feet in passing,
flickers of movement - imagined (or not . . .) - cause
eyes to squint
bodies to crouch
and necks to crane.

Stags, anxious not to awaken those
who sleep as babes
by jumping at the nocturnal movements
of dust,
quell their imaginations, breathe deeply, and settle down to watch
again.

Though shifts change,
worries stay.

Soldiers - girl and boy, man and woman -
think;
of loved ones
of rugby
of books
of music
of food
of sleep, all of which are denied them
for now,
all whilst watching for changes in the movements
of dust.

As morning's sun peeks
over distant mountains,
bodies - live, all -
stir.

They are lucky.
They are whole.

Cold, grey, harsh light,
probing
into every nook of camp,
breaks even the deepest slumber.

All live to see the
cold, grey, harsh light,
thanks to sleepless brothers -
and sisters -
at arms.

Sleepless.
Soundless.
Peerless.
Watching and listening
through night's vast aloneness.

Eyeing
swirling gusts
and gusting swirls -
eddying motions of the nocturnal movements
of dust.

Rhodri Williams (17)

VFM

We are the coin of war
With which another few feet of earth,
Another broken building
Or another stretch of stinking water
Can be bought.
They sent us here to die
And die we did.
For we, the coin of war
Were sent.
Now we are spent

RIP.

Adrian Yates

My Soul Knows

Comfort me, my darling!
Caress my lips with care,
In your arms, embrace me!
My soul knows solace there.

Doubtful and distrustful
Of people everywhere,
In your arms, I'm certain,
My soul knows true love there.

Though this life is fleeting,
No fear of loss I bear,
In your arms eternal,
My soul knows I'll be there.

Kate Miller

The Old Soldier

'T'wer never like this when I were a lad.'
The old soldier used to say.
'Had to do what I were told
no nonsense in my childhood day.'
Of his service days he never spoke.
A portion of his life that was kept
deep within, only reappearing in
dreadful dreams, whilst he slept.

He dreamt of his home so far away,
of his loving wife and son.
He dreamt of noise and blood and gore
of when this war was done.
As a youth he fought for God and King
and something he could never understand;
how he came to lose his precious wife and son
whilst he fought in foreign lands.

So now he lives by manners and rules of old,
and tells how things were then.
But you won't be told how bad it was.
How the war took boys and made them men.
He keeps the memories of his wife and son,
of comrades who beside him fell.
And perhaps he listens to other
souls who have sad tales to tell.

'T'wer not like this when I were a lad.'
Is how *his* story goes.
He doesn't say his life was sad,
he thinks nobody knows.
His rheumy eyes may look back on life,
but no words are ever said.
Because he can never speak
of the type of youth he led.

Mary Howcroft

That Hooded Figure

Slowly, quietly from the fog
A gangly shadowy figure appears
Thin and frail it is, but deadly
Death roams the Earth
A sickle as its sceptre
Door by door it knocks
But one can stop this messenger
Through the power of God the creator
There is a due date and time
That cannot be stopped by dimes
When that hooded figure
Indeed a devilish part of nature
Comes to collect on its appointment
It cannot be escaped by sinful Man
When to be it was meant
But eternal death can be trampled
Under the cover of the almighty
Life forever more is assured
Not by our power but by God's might
We have overcome death
By the blood of the lamb.

Debra Ayis

Nature Has No Seasons

Orphaned leaves
court the brown season
in streets calm with houses
where procession passes
in fullness and grief

it is a time when Earth shall
take back its budding spring
pack up the sun of summer
and look to winter's way

chilled in this season
berries red for Christmas
the mighty spiked mahonia
and all of hamamelis
with spicy scented flowers

what of Man
and timely seasons
when all of time
is nature's need?

George Carle

Choices

The child born out of passion
And lustful desires,
Stands forlorn

The child conceived out of love
And the bond of family ties,
Stands beside him

The feast eaten noisily with strangers
To satisfy an alcoholic hunger,
Pollutes all who partake of it.

The simple meal lovingly prepared
And eaten in good company,
Satisfies both body and soul.

The life enacted out devoid of depth
Of thought, or future plans, is going
Only to a miserable end.

The life that's lived in earnest
With dreams and goals of high endeavour
Will surely be fulfilled.

The world that's filled with greed and anger,
With hatred, fear and wrong desires
Must surely die.

The world renewed, with peace and love
The only true religion, where deities walk the Earth
Will surely yet arise.

The time for change and new beginnings
Is upon us each and every one.
Who will take up the challenge and make the choices
Before a new day has begun?

Will it be you, or I? Or shall we wait yet again
To see what happens? And drown in a tsunami
Of ignorance, because we didn't even try!

William Ross

The Wrong Return For Service

Do you remember playing with coloured lead soldiers?
Do you remember lining them up in fighting files?
Do you remember the pitched battles and the wounded galore?
Do you remember the flagpole and standard always flying?
The childhood dreams.

Did you always yearn to wear the uniform?
Did you always stand up straight with badges pronounced?
Did you always know it would give you an adrenaline boost?
Did you always feel proud knowing what it represented?
It's all in the wearing.

So when the time came, you marched to the danger lands.
So when the time came, you marched into Ireland.
So when the time came, you marched into Iraq.
So when the time came, you marched into Afghanistan -
Yours was not to question the why.

And you came back home with legions of memories
And you came back home with a job nearly satisfactorily done
And you came back home smothered in glory
But sadly you came back home covered by a Union Jack,
Receiving the nation's grateful thanks
And a burial with full military honours.
The harsh reality of modern life.

Robert Main

Ghosts

I see the ghosts of soldiers,
I knew so long ago.
In hazy dreams of far off days
Seeing them in so many ways,
On parade, listening to what the sergeant says.
In the NAFFI, drinking, singing, cursing.
On the field of battle, waiting to give their all.
The deadly hush before the battle starts,
The pounding heart as the shells begin to fall.
I am scared and he is too.
When I turn - my pal has gone.
But all this is in a dream.
And this morning is warm and sunny
But not for my pal, he gave his all.

G B Taylor

The Music At Cwmdu

The music at Cwmdu is glorious
It's live on the first Friday night
The trumpet is waiting implorious
With practice the notes come out right

It's live on the first Friday night
With a story, a strum and a joke
With practice the notes come out right
But it's outside to light up a smoke

With a story, a strum and a joke
And a beer that comes straight from a bottle
It's outside to light up a smoke
The dulcet becoming quite glottal

And a beer that comes straight from a bottle
Finds a way to go straight to the head
The dulcet becoming quite glottal
And the rondel becoming quite dead

Finds a way to go straight to the head
With the night leaning more to notorious
And the rondel becoming quite dead
The music at Cwmdu is glorious!

Anton Leslie

A Lost Flower

When a daffodil tilted
And eventually fell into the stream
There was a subtle sigh
In the grasses nearby.

Around a stone, the blossom
Briefly lingered as though waiting
For a friendly hand to put
Her back on land. But the rain
Came and whisked her away
Downstream, a bright yellow
Memory of what might have been.

Robert Wynn-Davies

Hope For Humanity

I sit and ponder hour by hour,
Despairing at the state
Of people round the world today
And how they don't relate
To any of the principles
We always held so dear,
Yet seem to find the strangest things
So obvious and clear.

Each day goes by and I lament
The ever failing line
Of people and my hopes for us:
If only some could shine.
But so it happens, now and then,
And makes it all worthwhile,
A sense of pride that we achieve,
And do it with some style.

Instead of pressing self-destruct,
And choosing not to be
The slightest bit concerned with facts
Around us, that we see.
Just now and then folk show a side
So different to the norm,
That makes the disillusioned soul
Feel comforted and warm.

So when I sit there hour by hour
Downhearted and bereft
Of any hope for each of us, and
The lives that we have left,
I just hold on to that one thought:
Whatever now we do
To make believe there is no hope,
I know that we'll come through.

Helen Round

My Heart Is A Treasure

My heart is a treasure
Full of treasures
As big as the world
As wide as the sky
As deep as the sea
Sparkling with hidden gems
And warmth of sun
Rich and golden
Soft as snow
Beautiful as the breeze
Smell me in the summer
Touch me in the autumn
Hold me in the winter
For I am never far
I am a treasure you will
Never see
Feel me
I am universal love
Kissing your soul
Tickling your toes
Caressing your hair
And blessing your heart
For evermore.

Sian Boissevain

Forsaken Pearls

Thrown aside onto the coffee table, pearls pure as satin
A collection of mingling and clucking
As they land onto varnish, their shiny pebbles mound
One on top of another, piled high, embracing the paraphernalia
And two by two, white virginal bracelets are discarded
Joining their sisters as they line up for perusal
Their sweetness undiscovered, their jewels untouched,
Abandoned in their strung assembly.
Hours later, cold light crashes into sweet
Smelling hay; piles of it warm yet arrow-like,
The milk maids, lank curls pushed from tired eyes
Squeeze and pull, milk pure as pearls,
Gushes out - a mixture of suckling and longing.

Angie Davies

Pains Of War

Tell me of pain
The journalist asked
I thought
And then I replied
What kind of pain?
Is it that which is seen?
Or is it the pain from inside?

There's pain that is felt
In limbs that are gone
And also from flesh wounds and sores
But also the pain we feel in our head
When thinking of sights in the wars

There's pain that we feel
When we see a mate fall
And know they will never arise
And pain as we tell
The ones that were loved
How it happened in front of our eyes

There's pain that is felt
On waving goodbye
When duty once more makes its call
And loved ones must wait until we return
And pray that we make each roll call

There's pain that is felt
By those left behind
As hot tears their eyes and cheeks burn
Knowing full well that in life's cruel fate
It may be, you never return

And then there's the pain
When coming back home
To find that very few care
'Bout the problems we meet
In today's civvy street
When trying to settle back there

So please jot it down
In your notebook, my friend
There's many a story to tell
But there's not much to gain
When you tell of our pain
For people just don't seem to care.

Robert John Ponting

Beside The Sea - Arromanches
(Dedicated to my husband who is a veteran of the D-Day landings at Arromanches and who visited the beaches in 2009 on the 65th anniversary)

Beside the sea, one summer morn,
In waves they came and fell -
Fighting for others to be free.

Out of the mist and swell,
Sons and brothers, sweethearts
and fathers too, waded into hell.

They came ashore, boys but yesterday,
Suddenly made men,
United by a common cause.

They fought their gory battles
with selfless courage and determination,
To free a people and a nation.

Now, five and sixty years have passed,
And the gallant dwindling few,
Remember well, their fallen comrades.

'Veterans', designated, they come
in fewer and fewer numbers now,
To remember, the exploits of the gallant men.

Now old and bent and frail,
With rheumy eye and memory long,
They shed a tear for comrades gone.

They lay their wreaths and poppies,
And say a prayer of thankfulness,
'I survived' the D-Day landings - beside the sea.

Vivian Barlow

A Father

A father is a strong man,
Whether he be short or tall.
So strong in his protection,
Who picks you up each time you fall . . .
Who fights your battles for you,
When you are small and weak.
Who loves you without judging,
When you begin to feel your feet . . .
Someone you are proud of,
Who is always on your side.
Lets you try all new things,
To open up your mind so wide . . .
To help you be so confident,
To stand on your own two feet.
When any sort of problem,
Through life, you may well meet . . .
Who loves you with such tenderness,
Will never let you down.
Even when you do things wrong,
And looks at you, and frowns . . .
You always know, that he'll be there,
When there's times, that stretch you thin.
And help you to regain your loss,
So that in the end, you'll win . . .
Let's think of what they mean to us,
And how much we love them too . . .
Let them know how much respect,
We feel, in all they do . . .
So when you're feeling down,
And you miss him, now you're grown.
Just let the memories, come flooding back,
Then you'll never feel alone . . .

Janet Starkey

Afghanistan Elegy

Slowly the cortege moved along
Bearing the coffin with the flowers upon,
And the women wept as the men looked on,
- Another soldier dead and gone.

How many more will be Taliban kills
As the army fights in the barren hills
Of that God-forsaken, lawless land,
That slaughterhouse, Afghanistan?

The enemy fights as if a shadow,
Here today and gone tomorrow,
Sniping with a deadly skill,
Picking off the men to kill.

Beside the road they're planting mines,
Carefully hidden, no outward signs,
And waiting till army trucks pass by
To blow the convoy up, sky high.

Thus we watch the Roll of Honour grow
With a feeling of despair,
For nobody appears to know
Why our boys are fighting there.

The Cabinet claims: 'for security',
But how can that be sanity,
When our border control is woefully slack,
Letting terrorists enter behind its back?

David J King

Penton; Goodbye

Will you walk with me, will you?
Will you take me in the sun
when long shadows
drift and dance behind us?
Will you take me down the lane
and through the fields?

Will you walk with me, will you?
Will you let me feel the corn
dress my legs with cobwebs,
caressing as we pass?
Will you take me by the village
while the sky glows red?

Will you walk with me, will you?
Will you take me past the woods
where whispers seep and melt
in the darkening trees?
Will you take me through the beeches
where the barn owls cry?

Will you walk with me, will you?
Will you take me home
along the path sunk deep and low
by feet trod centuries ago?
Will you lead me through the grass
all dark and damp with dew?

In the warm and gentle dusk,
once more, like summers past,
will you walk with me, will you?

Noele Mackey

One More Day

If I had one more day with you
We would have walked through a hundred English gardens
Whilst drenched in summer rain.
We would watch the golden sun climb up towards the skylark heavens,
Then smile as it stumbles back down,

Sit in awe as the swallows dance over the pebble-dashed cottages
Like tiny paper planes,
One more day to show you love, colour and joy,
To show you why children laugh out loud and play silly games.

I need these hours to see you when I was not looking,
To hear you when my ears were blocked,
To hold your hand when need not taking,
And smash the hour before the hour had clocked.

One more day to hold back the darkened tide,
That folds over us all when our time is up.
To touch your face and look at you with bloodshot eyes
And beg you for one last day to
Never give up.

Fariah Rahman

Send Them Home

How many more tears have to be shed?
How many more families are living in dread?
How many more funerals have to be held?
Send them home.

Golden Grove will be bought to show we care
For our wonderful heroes over there
We will make it a home to heal your pain
And in time you will feel complete again.

The heartache will fade a little each day
And bad memories will just fade away
And the valleys will rejoice when we can say
The boys are coming home.

Maureen Cole

Remembrance Day

Graveyard filled with identical crosses
Marks the spot of so many losses
Most of them still in their teens
Never to fulfil their young dreams

Poppies blowing in the breeze
People praying on their knees
Kneeling down before a cross
Remember the dead, remember their loss

The young ones who went to answer the call
Went into battle but bravely did fall
They did their best our country to save
Now just a name upon a grave

They fought for their country brave and bold
Young men never to grow old
Now just a face in a photograph
Never again to cry or laugh

The loved ones that they left behind
Walk through the graveyard until they find
The spot allotted to their kin
Who fought the war they tried to win

They did not ask or reason why
When asked to fight and maybe die
We owe them a debt we cannot repay
So please just honour them on this day.

William Meechan

Our Mother

Many years ago you left us
We tried so hard in vain
To keep you always with us
And free you from your pain

You made our lives so happy
And gave us lots of love
We know you're still watching over us
Even though it's from Heaven above

We prayed to God to help you
And He took you for a rest
We lost a wonderful mother
But He only picks the best.

Derek Gealy

Beloved Druggie

I was a good student, but couldn't sit still for long,
And this is my story of how it went wrong.
I went through primary, with brilliant grades,
Or that's what I remember, as my memory fades.
Secondary was harder, I was in the wrong crowd,
Always taking it further, to try and make them proud.
Wes was the one that got me into drugs,
I remember the night, we were out in a club,
When he got out a packet,
It was handed around,
With each different person, another ten pounds.
It was handed to me, and I looked at him blankly,
He said, 'It's only Es, lighten up little Andy!'
It was good at first, up and dancing with every song,
But not long after, things started to go wrong.
I stopped doing my homework, and bunked off class,
Most of the time, I took it at the back in maths.
Straight As turned to Bs, soon followed by Cs,
I think I started failing when I was taking weed.
I wasted all my money, and most of my short life,
Dealing drugs, when someone came at me with a knife.
Wanted free drugs, I think he was after a spliff,
He didn't intend to kill me, he must have just slipped,
But my dangerous addictions, and not being able to behave,
The drug dealing and taking, landed me in an early grave.
I was buried in my home town, in a quiet churchyard,
Where each week someone leaves flowers and a card.
Now I'm stuck, 19 forever, on my gravestone it says
'Beloved druggie, dealer, thief, only loved by Wes'.

Rebecca Farish

Ode To Wales

Listen! hear the red kite calling
high above the green Welsh hills,
See the white foamed falls a-tumbling,
spilling, flowing through the fields.

Golden daffodils are shining
as round our chapel yards they throng,
Feel the ancient breezes blowing
bringing tunes to harp and song.

Watch the Welsh black cobs a-galloping
hear the little lambs that bleat,
Taste the cheese made in these valleys
feed on cawl and bara-brith.

Shout with joy! as Wales is winning
in our nation's favourite game,
Keep a welcome in the hillside
to greet our tourist friends again.

Remember the Carmarthen shilling
keep alive the coracle crafts,
Weave a shawl for the baban
carve a spoon to help love last.

Hear the people speaking, singing
in their native tongue - cymraeg
Impassioned voices raised in anthem
'neath the dragon flag that flies.

Siwla Virago

Poppies

The conflict down to those that erred,
The excitement and glory of joining,
Patriotism, dented but not deterred,
Fear and anguish, slowly waning.

Far away, on foreign fields,
Memories of loved ones strong,
Dogged-eared photos concealed
Will we meet again, as in the song?

Autumn winds are sweeping
Across those desolate plains,
Dank days are shortening,
The mists, the chills, and the rains.

Soldiers, old and young, all brave,
The old remember earlier campaigns,
The young, learn their war, day by day,
And became old before their times.

The guns fall silent
As echoes shook the air,
Now, an eerie hush
Of softly spoken prayer.

The battle, now ended,
Giving thanks for coming through,
Soldiers, on knees bended,
Something reverent to do.

Elsewhere, on the battlefield,
Shell-shocked, blinded and numb,
Fallen comrades about to yield
Their final sigh, and then, succumb.

Autumn gold to winter white,
Trenches, troops, out of sight,
Frozen ruts and footprints deep,
Encased, beneath nature sleeps.

Winter thaws to reveal the spring,
Nature stirred, and breathed, rebirth,
In this pitted wilderness of suffering,
New growth, new life, budding forth.

Another season of renewal
First the green, and now the bloom,
Papery petals slowly unfurl,
Creased from being in a bud.

Fine and delicate, nodding to the sun
Whose warmth, the sails doth smooth,
Not a wayside weed, but an emblem,
A sign, the blood, that many did lose.

Across the wasteland, getting greener,
Swaying regal, a regiment of guards,
Poppies red, bloom for every season,
Petals glow with pride, fade to seed, to sleep.

Each stem a defender of the realm,
Each petal, revered, a sacrificed life,
Comrades, united, against the foe,
Mourned by parent, brother, sister or wife.

Memorials to the fallen, wreaths of red,
Walls with lists of names, 'The Glorious Dead',
Always November, remembrance in our hearts,
Honoured by the nation, noble deeds impart.

Jackie Domingo

The Killing Fields
(Dedicated to all the servicemen and women serving in Afghanistan)

Oh, when will all this terror end?
Of the maiming and killing of our fellow men.
With the slaying and bombing of innocent lives.
Of the emptiness left, within mothers and wives.
The killing of a hero is sad and tragic.
In a country so evil, and totally barbaric.
Our troops are there to combat peace.
Instead, they face terror and grief.
These evil acts of the Taliban.
In the killing fields of Afghanistan.
Limbs are lost in dreaded landmines.
Abandoned by the Russians a long past time.
Many lives have been lost by this senseless war.
There's no need for bloodshed anymore.
We're praying for victory for this war to be won.
Giving peace and harmony for everyone.
Praying and waiting for peace to be served.
A truly welcome home, our heroes deserve.

Catherine Fleming

Just Seventeen

You were just a young boy
Seventeen years old
You went away to fight a war
This story has been told

You fought beside the bravest
But tears would sometimes flow
Each time a mate had left you
You cried to see him go

Growing up was hard for you
Living in the mud
Down inside cold trenches
Where you saw the sight of blood

So many times you prayed to God
Please take me away from here
But somehow time was turning
Into another year

You were just a young boy
When you went away
But you are now a grown-up man
My son, what can I say?

I never meant for you to see
The things that you have seen
You went away far too young
A boy of seventeen.

Florence Davies

Soldier Soldier

As I sat on my mother's knee
I looked up at her smiling face looking down at me.
Her hand caressed my golden hair,
As she held me close and tight as ever,
And said, 'You are my little soldier.'

In my teens I joined the Army,
To be a real soldier.
Dressed in camouflage and beret
I waved goodbye to my loving mother.

Afghanistan was a place I'd seen on telly,
Being there was really frightening.
Dust and grit blew into my face,
What am I doing in this place?
My kit was heavy as we trudged over rough terrain,
Tanks and guns making grinding noises,
Looking for the enemy.

We never talked or thought of danger,
Kept chins up and heard some laughter.
Roadside bombs killed some friends,
Is it ever going to end?

Alas my time was up, the end was near.
Blown and injured as I'd feared,
Everything turned to night.
The silence like a floating cloud.
No voices shouting out aloud.

I saw my mother's face was crumbling,
Her caressing hands were trembling.
No longer able to hold me tight
And call me her little soldier.
I had lost my life in the fight
To make another country better.

E Evans

Lewis George

Lewis George is a one-eyed duck
He's a very good friend of mine
Doesn't seem to have much luck
Caught his leg in a fishing line.

Lewis George has only one wing
He finds it difficult to walk
Likes to think that he can sing
But all he does is squawk.

Lewis George is a friend of mine
Thought he was a lady
Went and sat on a chicken egg
Thought he'd hatch a baby.

Lewis George is a one-eyed duck
He's a very happy soul
Likes to swim around and around
Like a goldfish in a bowl.

Jeanne Evans

How Time Flies

It only seems like yesterday
That I was still at school
Listening to my teachers
And sometimes playing the fool

Then when I was in my teens
It was make-up, clothes and boys
I left behind my younger days
And finished with my toys

Then after school I found a job
To try and earn some money
Often times were very hard
It was not all milk and honey

Now that I am getting old
With the years swiftly passing away
I look back on the life I've had
And thank God for every day

Pat Gealy

Hold On

At times I don't understand
The need to fight
At times I don't understand
Why you want to fight
I understand the reason but
I can never understand you

Am scared, scared of losing
You my friend, my lover, my rock
And though my heart aches
Am still proud of who you are

Hold on, just hold on
In your eyes, I see strength

In your heart you may be scared
But hold on to your truth
It's what you know
It's what you live for

Fear grips me every day
My soul is never at peace
My spirit filled with worry
Every part of me is missing you

Am scared, scared of losing
You my friend, my love, my rock
And though my heart aches
Am still proud of who you are

Hold on, just hold on
In your eyes, I see strength
In your heart, you may be scared
But hold on to your truth
It's what you know
It's what you live for.

Adwoa Asiedu

Help!

I've got a new car
Now my poor brain I rack
To know what and where the gadgets are
But, oh I'd love my old car back!

The new car's manual is so technical
It's all gobbledegook to me
And by the time I've tried to sort it out
I'm barking mad up a tree!

It really is a wonderful book
Of technology, with drawings superb
But sometimes the words that I say about this book
Should never, ever be heard!

I know it's there to help me
Of that there is no doubt
But try as I might - and I really do try
I cannot make it out.

Yesterday I drove to Tesco's
To do my monthly shopping
I felt in charge as the car moved off
No worry about starting or stopping.

On getting home the shopping I removed
Then into the garage drove the car
Switching on the headlights to judge the distance
To the back wall - I cannot go in too far.

Superbly driven, I congratulate myself
And locked the car up for the night
But next morning the car would not start
No response! Panic stations! What a fright!

What have I done? - I've spent all that money
For a car that's not working today.
I phoned the dealers, could they come and help?
They said, yes, they would come right away.

They kept to their word and were soon on the scene
But the car was perfectly alright
The fault was mine - I had switched on the lights,
And left them on all night!

The battery was flat, it would have to be recharged
The knowledge of this car I lack
More money I must pay to have this trouble sorted,
So please, please, bring my old car back!

Doris Steere

My Job

(To Gregg Stevenson and Ben Parkinson)

My legs blown off
As I stood on
An explosive
Signed *Taliban*
On the dusty mountainous soil.

Saved by comrades . . .
. . . Today . . .
With prosthetic legs
As I look for
Mines and explosives

The agony of comrade Ben
Echoes louder than
Posh bombs
On the dusty mountainous soil
In his multi-fractured
Legless body.

Brinda Runghsawmee

Where Is He?

Where is he, that little boy
That looks out from the frame,
All tousled hair and cheeky grin
As if wanting to play a game?

He was here, just a moment ago
Surely I can't be wrong?
We were talking and laughing
And snuggling up - it doesn't seem that long.

Why, it was only yesterday
That he burst home from school
With wrinkled socks and news to tell
Of how he'd swum his first strokes in the pool.

Yes, it was only yesterday
That he fell asleep in my arms
With his thumb in his mouth
And Teddy, keeping him from harm.

So where is my boy, where has he gone?
Is he upstairs in his bed?
Is he perhaps with his toy cars in the sandpit,
Or building a garage for Ted?

Perhaps he is out in the garden,
Making a camp or a den,
With a sheet flung over the washing line
As a hideout for friends, David and Ben.

Perhaps that's him,
Over there, by the wall,
It reminds me of him
But he's grown very tall.

The hair is not so blond
And it's spiked out with gel.
He wears smart long trousers,
And they fit him so well.

He smiles as he sees me
And although the light's dim,
Do I really detect stubble
On that familiar chin?

Is this man my boy?
My sweet, precious son?
He can't be that age surely,
For only yesterday he was young.

Penny Gillman

Fear Of Love

Love has taken hold of me, it's touched my very soul
Deep within the core of me and it just won't let me go
In bliss is what I should feel now but fear of being hurt
Is what seems to be the focus point of this love which has occurred

I wonder if we truly know what love is all about
Maybe an experience we will never learn about
This love which I have waited for should make my heart feel pure
But all it seems to do to me is cause me far more hurt

Is love a fear, a doubt in mind, an emotion to cause pain
And doubt in one's ability to ever trust again
With love it makes us vulnerable and open to one's fears
Not knowing if it's right or wrong or if it will succeed

Although this love I've waited for, for such a long, long time
Has brought about my fears of doubt and that I can't deny
I've wanted all the joys of love the dreams and hopes to come
But now it's split emotions of fear and hurt that shows

I'm scared of love, I know this now a fear of letting go
To give myself completely, my body, heart and soul
To put my trust in someone else, to let my feelings flow
This fear of being hurt by them will crush my very soul

But love it has a hold of me, I know not what to do
I search my heart, my soul complete for answers which are true
But fear is there, it stands so strong it will not go away
I thought that love would conquer all and let me live again.

Amanda Griffith

Heroes And Hearts

With heavy hearts we watch them leave
Tears and fears, God watch over them please
With baited breath we wait at home
knowing they're out there all alone

We pray to God to keep them safe
while they're fighting for the human race
help them keep their faith, your Grace
for we long to see our loved one's face

How hard it is to be apart
from those we hold in our heart
Heroes each and every one
A daughter, sister, brother, son

We thank you
each and every one.

Sue Harries

Come Home

Come home,
But not before you've stopped
the fear
in children's eyes.

Come home,
But not before you've won
the war
for women's freedom
and education.

Come home
But not before
you have restored
a better way of living.

But come home safe,
Come home.

Hilary Sauvarin Cackett

Repatriation

Stand in line with all heads bowed.
Eyes may weep but hearts are proud.
Stand by, and still as they pass by.
Keep to yourself the wonder why.

Stand in line you men of rank
and pray to God and Him do thank.
Salute the lost. Salute them all.
Salute them all, the ones that fall.

Be witness to the bloody truth
where our young men betray their youth.
When they return with life expired
'neath Union flag, forlorn and tired.

Wootton Bassett bears the name.
A town that holds a grievous fame.
Where flowers are left where feet should be
and echoed cries are heard. Set free.

Stand in line you commons folk
and share the burden of their yoke.
Remember them that you did send.
Remember hearts that you did rend.

Kin folk weep for all your loss.
Bless your brave child and bear the cross.
Stand strong for those no longer there.
A nation's grief, with you, we'll share.

Margaret Edge

In This Life

In this life, when death has left its mark,
Free-falling into the abyss I go,
Weightless, but with a heavy heart,
Where it is blacker, than the darkest night
You are not there.
I know not where you are.
You do not share my feelings of helplessness and solitude.
Alone, I claw my way from this empty space.
From this hard place in my mind.
Back to this life.
Out of nowhere, I hear a whisper that says,
'Try again, my love, live your life, and try again for my sake.'

Ann Holland

Our Light Fantastic

In ripe-cherry rapture
I picked a sugar-spun star
from the sky that we shaped,
when we created the world.
My hand tingled as I pulled,
a radiant wave of rhapsody
pulsating through fingers and bone,
hairs prickling as if minuscule crabs
were nipping a pathway to the sea.
It beamed pink and rainbow in my palm,
sweetly beating heart
of a Crayola factory.

Bathing in colour that was ours,
we were whirlybugs waltzing in its glow,
light as spidery silken thread.
Caught in a hypnotic hue,
we danced until dizzy, like thieves
who'd fleeced a Fabergé egg.
And, as the stars' shine
slowly dimmed to a shimmer in my hand,
astral body crumbling
into day-glow dust,
we looked to the sky again,
and it was your turn to pick,
from that infinite celestial trust.

Andrea Wren

Skin

Layers, tiers, tears.
The chronological thickening of skin.
Is it a sin?
To be so outwardly jagged, canvas white
In this spell, the age of passion's fiery bite?

I might
Wear it down, crumble, flake
to find that natural ache
and re-awaken gushing trust
that thrusts towards crimson-cheeked brain-blindness,
mistrust in concentrated kindness,
to undress the core of its shadows
and reveal the monsters, in their tedious magnificence.

But should it be swathed,
plastered, rusted over and dulled a sophisticated grey?
Modest and hidden.
Shoulders protectively slumped,
making me stumped
in the face of unconditional affection.

Understand it's a reaction
to a reflection.

Rebecca Taunton

Sleep

I settled down in bed last night
And closed my weary eyes
I tried to clear my mind of thoughts
But much to my surprise
Though shattered from a hectic day
With aching limbs, so sore
My mind was flitting back and forth
But why? Why now? What for?
I tossed and turned, removed the sheet
My body's hot, I've got cold feet
Should I get up and make a drink
Or will that mean more time to think?
A gentle elbow in the ribs
Put paid to snoring from 'his nibs'
He seemed oblivious to my plight
His body knew that it was night
I then decided counting sheep
Would probably send me off to sleep
It didn't help, the time rolled by
But then I thought 'a lullaby'
It worked in childhood, why not now?
It did the trick, don't ask me how
Next thing, I heard the alarm clock ringing
I had found sleep by gently singing.

Averil Fairey

Gulf War Special
(For Dave)

'Oh it will all be very jolly when we ship you off to war
Cos Hussein's a cruel bully and it's time he was no more.
With your call-up papers posted, pack your kit and oil your gun,
And we'll ship you to the desert - you'll enjoy a bit of sun.'

Anthrax jabs, Malaria tabs,
Boil up your billy for your rat-pack bag.
Things don't look so bad as we're firing on Baghdad.
Can't wait to see Kuwait -
How far's Basra?

Scorpion hider and camel spider
Back in the pan where our tents all stand
And the sandstorm's power strips paint and skin.
There's times I'd like to jack it in.

But I really should be thankful
For we've spare parts by the tankful
And a shower-bag that's hot - though soap there's not!
For the lass who's my best mate - or
My germ proof respirator
And the blueys from back home
Which keeps me sane.

'Cept as I dig another hole
For one more mutilated soul,
I'll be glad when we are shipped back home again.

Yvonne Brunton

2010

Experience the loneliness
Wrap yourself in the fear
Where time is but an echo
Of a family no longer near

Clinging onto photographs
Words infrequently spoken
Letters worn, ink blurred
Too many young hearts broken

Drifting scenes of childhood
But memories of the past
Images of togetherness
Disappearing fast

Dreams now seen as fairy tales
Tears have all run dry
Mothers' sons are dying
As 'Leaders' fail to try.

Claire Morris

Degradation

Empty pages from empty books
Empty faces giving empty looks
No one bothers, no one cares
No one tries because no one dares
Lack of feeling, lack of thought
Why is the answer always nought?
No one running only ambling
Not talking sense only rambling
Never happy always sad
Never good but only bad
Empty colleges, empty schools
No one cares about the rules
Closed down libraries and seats of learning
Nothing to spend because no one's earning
Overgrown gardens full of overgrown weeds
Lack of knowledge because no one reads
From empty pages . . .

Trevor Foster

To Fallen Heroes

When the days lengthen
And scented flowers bloom,
When wispy clouds float onward
And drag away the gloom,

Oh my heart cries out for you.

When autumn comes I'll think of you
Amid the tall trees' coloured hue,
Where raindrops carelessly alight,
And fall from branches silvery white,

And oh my heart cries out for you.

When dusk is seen in all its gloom
I pray you've only left the room,
Or maybe you have gone away
Or to the pub - another day,

And oh my heart cries out for you.

It seems so long since I saw your smile
Or heard your voice in a little while,
Or felt your breath as you were near,
Don't watch my tears,
Oh no my dear.

For oh my heart cries out for you.

It's Christmas now and the tree is bare,
The baubles are broken,
There's no one to care,
No presents wrapped in ribbons of red,
No crown upon the angel's head,

And oh my heart cries out for you.

Never will I forget you,
That someone loyal and oh so true,
Who touched my life with sapphires of blue,
Now days are shortened without you.

Yet still my heart cries out for you.

I pray that we will meet once more,
When Heaven opens up its door.
The brightest star will shine on me
And together we will always be,

Reunited in eternity.

Hannah Hall

Invisible Friend
(Dedicated with love to Adam, Mark, Frances, Dylan, Kayleigh and Chloe)

Her mother called, she didn't stir
School held no happiness for her
Her nightmares reflecting reality
She was nothing and would never be
But in her dreams, ah, she was loved
She wasn't scoffed at, pushed or shoved

Longing for peace, she played a game
Lifted high to another plane
In her trance state she was content
No abuse or to Coventry sent
The game had to end as all games must
She had to live life but lose all trust

No one to turn to, deserted she stood
Confiding in teachers was misunderstood
Her tormentors supreme, their victory won
For her every second was like when it begun
No respite, her ordeal didn't disappear
It just got worse year after year

She couldn't see any hope in sight
Ending it all she thought she just might
She lumbered home one day from another ordeal
She wished her pain someone could feel
Sitting on her bed contemplating the end
And wishing she had just one friend

Then a voice whispered softly in her ear
She looked around gripped with fear
But she didn't have to be afraid
She knew by his smile a friend she'd made
He took her hand holding it lovingly
Oh please don't let go she heard herself plea

The strength that flowed from him to her
Made her cry with relief and her heart soar
She knew that with him close by her side
He'd stem the tears she constantly cried
He taught her how to love herself
And of goodness and love she had a wealth

From then on at school as he gripped her hand
She took control as they had planned
She faced her tormentors with his hand in hers
She saw only envy exude from their pores
Her stature grew, she gained in height
They knew from then on to just keep quiet

He had rescued her from a place of dread
To a life filled with confidence instead
Now raised high above she looked down on the horde
Who had ruled her life and completely controlled
His hand slipped from hers, it was quite weird
His job complete as he just disappeared

Barbara Lambie

Willow Tree Night And Snowy Visitors

Winter tapping
hollow willow tree trunk -
a four month visitor about to move in
unload his messy clothing
be windy about it -
bark is grayish white as coming night with snow
fragments the seasons.
The chill of frost lays a deceitful blanket
over the courtyard greens and coats a
ghostly white mist over yellowed willow
leaves widely spaced teeth -
you can hear them clicking
like false teeth
or chattering like chipmunks
threatened in a distant burrow.
The willow tree knows the old man
approaching has showed up again,
in early November with
ice-packed cheeks and brutal
puffy wind whistling with a sting.

Michael Lee Johnson

Give That Little Bit More

When you wake up in the morning and you hear the birds sing
And music playing softly on the air, oh what joy it brings
Then imagine listening to the sobs of a child crying as it sits,
Eyes wide with horror, as it watches its
Mother dying from Aids with no money to pay for relief
In this day and age, it beggars belief
That those countries so rich won't cancel world debt
And tyrants grab and spend on themselves what monies they get
We all have a duty to do what we can,
Be we working class, celebrity, child, woman or man.

Give a little; give that little bit more, to the countries that are really poor
See the difference just a penny makes, give it for the little children's sakes
Medicines to help the sick and ill, grow the grain and empty bellies fill
Bricks and mortar; see the shelters grow, drill for wells and watch the water flow

If you've got that little extra at the end of the day,
Don't put it in your pocket, why don't you pay
It into a charity to put to good use
And help some small child who has faced abuse.
When you're sitting in comfort and the lights are low,
Think of all the homeless with no place to go.
When you hear your children's laughter and a smile crosses your face,
Think of the little one from a poorer race
Ravaged and savaged and left for dead,
Sores and flies surrounding its head.

Give a little; give that little bit more, to the countries that are really poor
See the difference just a penny makes, give it for the little children's sakes
Medicines to help the sick and ill, grow the grain and empty bellies fill
Bricks and mortar; see the shelters grow, drill for wells and watch the water flow

When you clear your table at the end of a meal,
See the waste you're leaving and think that some small child would steal,
Just to eat what you don't want and you throw it in the bin,
To us a daily habit, to the poor a sin.
When you buy that bar of chocolate and that extra treat,
Think of the child deprived with no energy to stand on its own two feet
Begging and pleading for a morsel or two,
Skin so transparent with its bones showing through.

Give a little; give that little bit more, to the countries that are really poor
See the difference just a penny makes, give it for the little children's sakes
Medicines to help the sick and ill, grow the grain and empty bellies fill
Bricks and mortar; see the shelters grow, drill for wells and watch the water flow

We have treasures and luxuries galore
And still we selfishly ask for more.
Rich kids' endless talk of fashion,
Poor kids, a bowl of rice to ration.
Look at yourself, what have you got, what can you give?
A little from everyone can help a poor child to live.

Give a little; give that little bit more, to the countries that are really poor
See the difference just a penny makes, give it for the little children's sakes
Medicines to help the sick and ill, grow the grain and empty bellies fill
Bricks and mortar; see the shelters grow, drill for wells and watch the water flow

Let's all unite and embrace Africa's sorrow,
And together help them build a new tomorrow.

Kal Elias

Pressed Man

Carried clearly across the water
mournful keening of paired seagulls.

In every direction the sea dominated,
winter-hard, blue-grey.

Starless night broken on occasion
by flashes of white wave.

Lantern-lit caverns on gloomy mess-decks
positively tomb-like.

Grey oatmeal mixed with black flecks
suggestive of darker secrets.

Air thickened with musty odour
of many men, the creeping fetor

of binge smells, moaning, coughing,
the weeping of obscenities.

Mighty beams sweeping, wrist-thick
ropes breeching guns.

Cruel cold wind blasting against
sodden clothing, reddening cheeks.

White gloves, gold-laced cocked hat,
the Captain disappeared below.

Beverly Maiden

Give Respect

Give respect where respect is due
especially to those who are good to you
the ones with the helping hand to lend
when things go wrong and you need a friend.

Give respect to those who care
and all your joys and troubles share
the friends we see most every day
who join us in our work and play.

Give respect to those who love
the gifts that come from above
the priest who prays that we be safe
in the words of wisdom, truth and faith.

Give respect to those who make
our lives more bearable for our sake
the doctor who restores our health
for health does not respect itself.

Give respect for mirth and song
which most great artists bring along
they give us pleasure every day
which cheerfully helps us on the way.

Give respect to those who use their skills
especially for those away from home
fighting for our country, we bless them all
and keep them safe till they return home.

Sylvia Quayle

Poppies

Poppies haphazardly patterned
Across a Flanders Field
Each one a fallen soldier's
Spirit living on.

Vicky Stevens

Springtime

It's spring, and time for birthing new lambs
They're so cute and so fluffy, just oozing with charm
We all want to see them and visit the farm
But hang on, we won't see them grow, and I fear
They're chosen for market before they're a year.

What makes us think, we have any more right
To live 'til we're ninety, and losing our sight
Bones creaking, hair falling and wrinkles galore
Bet the poor lambs wouldn't know us for sure!

Rabbits are lucky if they survive on the road
Crossing at night, can be awfully risky
But no one told them not to feel frisky
It's spring after all, and in the next valley
They might meet the one they're destined to marry!

Foxes are happy to see better weather
Their cubs have a chance of survival
If only some scraps can be nicked from the rival
Pet dogs are spoilt, but we all wish them well
They're set free from a scavenging hell.

So we all keep on trying to reach our potential
And know that spring will bring some fresh air
To our lives full of hope and mostly set fair
If only we're lucky and work hard to achieve
Just try not to think of those too early to leave.

Christine Weatherley

A Splash In A Puddle

A splash in a puddle of life that is all that we are
Some of the ripples that we make, never seem to get that far
They simply seem to fade away along with our wildest dreams
But we are hoping that our next one won't run out of steam.

We are hoping that they will carry us onto some sunny shore
But those ripples fade out and all about us is calm once more
Then we turn and look skyward to see the trail of a shooting star
Then we realise we are only a 'splash in a puddle' of life, that's all that we are.

By: 'The Dreaded Purple Fork'
alias
Mr Philip Anthony Amphlett

Maenad

She appears one night from the woods,
a pale and pretty thing.
A stranger to the campsite,
she simply begins dancing.

The Welsh mountains watch her,
unperturbed and unimpressed,
weightier things on their minds
than a woman barely dressed.

But others can't help but wonder
as she flits about with ease,
in the cold land of the dragon,
how is it that she does not freeze?

The thin metal walls of the caravan
echo and clang and shake,
playing chorus to the kinds of sounds
that no girl or beast should make.

The shrieks and yells and songs
that come unbidden from her throat
fly out on the same wind that whips
around her like a bitter winter coat.

And even as the tourists fear her,
this wild and beautiful creature,
they marvel at her set of lungs,
surely leant by Mother Nature.

Her beauty is a primal thing,
giddy on wine and bloodied furs;
for no hare nor fox nor doe
has feet as quick as hers.

She sways and spins alone,
observed from tents and camper vans,
yet those who watch her do not feel
it is a lonely dance.

Rather, she is surrounded by partners
they simply cannot see;
base and elemental beings that make her laugh
and hug herself with glee.

Some shed their clothes to join her,
to writhe and chant by her side.
She greets each one like a lover,
and begins to glow, lovely as a bride.

When men and women fall on each other
and the dance become a fray,
the maenad laughs and claps her hands,
then merrily runs away.

Her white body is visible for miles,
her cries heard wide and far.
Her glittering eyes mad, rapt and alive
with the light of the morning star.

Philip Ellis

Tears Of Pride

The day that he was born
She cried,
Tears of joy, tears of happiness and tears of pride.
She watched him grow from babe to child
And cried,
Tears of joy, tears of happiness and tears of pride.
The years rolled by and life did change,
A soldier he became.
She smiled and hugged him tightly,
Tried hard to hide her pain.
And then she cried,
Tears of joy, tears of fear and tears of pride.
That fateful day did happen
The one that she did dread,
He lost his life in battle
But with strength she raised her head
And cried
Tears of woe, tears of sorrow and many tears of pride.

Gaynor Morris

But Instead Has Gone Into Woods

A girl goes into the woods
and for what reason
disappears behind branches
and is never heard from again.
We don't really know why,
she could have gone shopping
or had lunch with her mother
but instead has gone into
woods, alone, without the lover,
and not for leaves or flowers.
It was a clear bright day
very much like today.
It was today. Now you might
imagine I'm that girl,
it seems there are reasons. But
first consider: I don't live
very near those trees and my
head is already wild with branches.

Lyn Lifshin

Colours Shared

There is a passion
That burns deep within
Stirs my soul
As angels sing
Your beauty
It commands a song
With words so simple
But never wrong
Time stands still
When you're around
Restless feet
On stony ground
As I await
A kiss from you
Colours shared
But never blue

Samantha Williams

Happy Family. Not!

18 years you were together,
15 years I came into your life forever.
Was I a mistake? I didn't care,
Into a happy, loving family my dreams were there.

October '08 the love ended . . .
Shouting, screaming, scrapping, shot through my ears
Messing with my brain.
I thought there was nothing to fear
But then you walked out . . .

You left me behind.
You didn't even say to my face goodbye.
B***h! I cursed when Dad told me,
Did you care that I wasn't there?
Depression, devastation, misery,
That's all that flowed through my body.
My heart was dying beginning to melt.
Tears flooded down my face,
When I looked at photos of us in a happy place.
'Kids always come first,' that's what you said,
I believed you until the rumours spread.

Dad, Grandma, Grandad and friends are the people that really care.
Even though I know you're always there
It's not the same, it will never be
I've got to move on; I've got to be free.

Jade Louise Piggott (16)

A Married Love
(Dedicated to my husband Antony)

For my husband, who I just want to say,
How much I love you, not just for today,
I've vowed to love you, with all my heart,
Through dark and cloud, to never part,
You're my one and only special baby,
I'm always gonna be your shining lady,
You deserve every day to be told,
That I love you forever, with this heart of gold.

Abigail Donoghue

Thoughts On Moving To Llanddowror

Listen to the whisper of the water by the willow,
Listen to the buzzing of the ever busy bee.
Listen to the lowing of the cattle in the meadow,
Listen to the country and relax along with me.

See the sweeping swallows bringing promise of the springtime,
See the modest primrose and the violet so shy,
See the little calves, the newborn lambs upon the hillside,
See the country, see the beauty, let the world go by.

Come now, leave the city life, the hassle and the stresses,
Where the days pass peacefully, there's time to stand and stare,
Watch the changing seasons, see the Earth don many dresses,
Here for city dwellers, is the answer to a prayer.

Dorothy Moody

Sayonara Soldier

Sadness overtakes me, when another soldier dies.
For protecting of the innocent, tears stream from their families' eyes.
How long should we allow, terror to take the lead
Democracy be denied, cruel practices to proceed?
Surely there comes a time, when good people must intervene,
Murder and torture to stop, freedom reality . . . not a dream.
Surely Christ would say, help the weak and frail,
Defend these from all harm, or in caring we do fail?
How to achieve this Lord, without the use of force?
The bullies must be stopped, to what ends must we recourse?
Sometimes there is no option, and death it will ensue.
So I pray for all those suffering, and I ask this now of you
For dear friends from each of us, the Lord our love demands,
And our duty in this life, is to obey all He commands.

Cecilia Jane Skudder

Peace Of Mind

A warm summer breeze, eased its way through the trees,
As I lay, half asleep, by the stream.
It swept over my face, with an increase in pace,
As if seeking a place in my dream.

For the first time for days, in that warm sun and haze,
The tensions had less of a hold.
Quite close I could hear, a bee beating the air,
As it carried its load of sweet gold.

Then a sound - oh so near, grew so loud and so clear,
Far too strong for a bee, it would seem.
The noise that was made, from each steel throbbing blade,
Destroyed the frail walls of my dream.

I woke with a start, and the beat of my heart,
Picked up speed, as I looked up to see.
My hand went to my belt, but nothing was felt,
In the space where the weapon should be.

The wings thrashed the air, as the chopper grew near,
Then suddenly appeared overhead.
I rolled to one side; there was nowhere to hide.
I lay still with my heart full of dread.

But the machine flew on by, to reveal clear blue sky.
I sat up, the sweat soaking each pore.
Then a young voice cried, 'Dad! We'll be late at the 'pad.
Our helicopter takes off at four!'

I got to my feet, then remembered the treat,
That I'd promised my son earlier that day.
How long would it take, for my family's sake,
To drive these old devils away?

David Anderson

Daffodils

I love to see daffodils blowing in the breeze
As they take in the sun's rays, quietly with ease
It's the flower of Wales
All yellow and gold
To see them in flower is a sight to behold.
They give your heart a life
In these often somber times
To see something so perfect, simply blows your mind.
If only I could paint this lovely living treasure,
Then life to me would be such a pleasure.
To see them growing on these Welsh hills,
This is my tribute to the lovely daffodils.

Barbara Rees

Where Wild Blossom Blows

The soldiers in their tunic graves sleep
The bereaved in sombre attire weep
Lesser talk about wars deep
And then go to bed ears blind
To the Great silent kind.

Scribbler

My Old Pals

My old pals where are they now, I often sit and wonder
Some are asleep in distant lands, where once the guns did thunder
I've kept in touch with quite a few and love to reminisce
Of times we had together and pals we sorely miss
We see the state of the world today and wonder what's gone wrong
Was it all worth it? We often ask when we think of pals that are gone
To a better world we like to think, where peace is all around
Where perhaps one day we all will meet with comrades we found

Frank Tampin

The Hungry Hunter

I saw a young man
with eyes full of laughter.
His name was Deadly Dereky Dan
two little geese went following him after.

Some places he went, they were constantly there
poking into his jeans, crawling onto his chair.
Before him, behind him - such an epoxy pair.

'Don't you ever get tired as, day after day,
when two little tagalongs get in your way?'

He beamed as he shook his dim young head
and I'll forever remember the terms what he said.

'It's fine to obtain party that run when you run;
and giggle when you're happy and drone when you hum -
For I only have shadows.'

So the wild geese flew with the stars on their wings,
the owls are calm in the still of night,
And a nightingale sits on a twig as it sings.
The motion of swirls sparkled in strong sprite.

There's only a sizzle of a breeze in the trees,
For the air is crisp, so crisp it will snap,
and tonight for certain there will be a freeze.
At the slightest sound, sizzle or snap.

An owl glides slowly over the treetops.
It lies and surveys the forest floor,
It gradually loops around a tree and stops.
Awestruck by mystery and Woodley lore.

Hours in the darkness in the forest there's no hope
He yaps and the stillness is split with a knife,
And the wild young man now evokes what he stole.
Yet all else continues with no conflict or strife.

Yasmin Abukar Ahmed (15)

Sea Of Love

You can throw your anchor out alone,
It's firmly attached to me,
Everything that I love is deep beneath the sea,
The chain is taut and I'm holding on,
Fast and with all my heart,
One day you may understand,
And a future we can chart.
I'll drag you through the coral bed,
We'll destroy whatever's in our way,
But no matter how hard you pull,
The chain will always stay.
Holding tight is what we'll do
No one understands
What torrent the sea can put us through
And we stay firm beneath the sand.
On calmer seas upon the deck,
Winched up close and tight,
If you dive over, I'll be there,
You are always in my sight.

Suzanne Harding

Young - Fit - Fearless

Young - fit - fearless - as recalled by kith and kin
Soldiers killed in action - what a bloody sin
The returning injured - menaced, limbless, fractured
Medics wade through tears - everybody tortured
Praise be to rehab - relentless inventiveness
Mended warriors - collective single-mindedness.

Judith Roberts

The Black Mountain Centre - Brynaman

We have grown up under this mountain
Enjoyed the freedom that it brings,
Crossed its streams, clambered over rocks
And listened to the wind as it calls and sings.

Our ancestors helped build this place
Stone by stone and called it their home,
The pool and cinema are still going strong
Surrounding walks and views are awesome.

In the middle of our small village
Is an old infant's school of note,
Built of red bricks it can't be missed
Education it was always meant to promote.

It still does with great Zeal and flourish
Its aim is to inspire all and delight,
Given a new lease of life by locals
The place is open all day until late at night.

Whether you are walking or come by car
Pop in and see our grand heritage display,
The gallery of scenes painted locally
The jewellery and crafts skilfully moulded in clay.

Spend some time with us, we won't mind
Buy a sandwich and a cup of hot tea,
Or select a freshly cooked lunch
In our splendid looking restaurant and café.

So we have it all here in Welsh Wales
Come and see, smell, taste, touch it - you can!
We're waiting to welcome you
At the magnificent Black Mountain Centre - Brynaman.

Colin Jones

My Mum And Coffee
(For my mother, who is faultless and the person I depend on the most)

In the morning my mum is picky,
about how her coffee is,
She doesn't like it from a SodaStream,
because it'll have way too much fizz!
She won't drink it if the milk used
is gold-top or full fat,
She doesn't like it with brown sugar,
believe me that is that!
She won't drink it if I make it
with boiled water, 'It is too hot!'
She doesn't like it from a paper cup,
or from a coffee pot.
She hates it when it's instant,
or if it doesn't have enough heat,
She doesn't like it when it's bitter,
or if it's very, very sweet!
She won't have a cup between a meal,
She doesn't drink coffee in bed,
So usually in the morning
she'll have some tea instead!

Maria Dixon

Childminder

What does she do when I've gone home?
Does she sit there all alone?
Does she put the teddies to bed
Or does she sit there scratching her head?
Does she read a book to herself
Or does she leave it on the shelf?
Does she bathe the goldfish
Or does she leave them in the dish?
Does she finish all the jigsaws
Or does she go outside and play on the see-saw?
Does she put all the toys away
Ready for another day?

Stephanie Rees (10)

Once A Grenadier

When I joined the Grenadiers I became unique
When I joined the Grenadiers I became special

They talked about the Blue, Red, Blue
And about it running through and through

Now I've left the Grenadiers I'm still unique
Now I've left the Grenadiers I'm still special

Now I talk about the Blue, Red, Blue
And about it running through and through

It's true to say that once you're a Grenadier
You're always a Grenadier

And that the Blue, Red, Blue
Will run through and through

Neil Young

Swift

The wind blew slow
The grass waving gently in the summer breeze
The sun dipped low behind a hill
And the pink light rained across the land
A swift dipped low dancing on the wind
Its wings beating; inches from the ground
One way; then the next, darting from left to right
And the pink light rained across the land
Another swift joins the flight
Swooping low; weaving, together in perfect harmony
Then they split up; one heading for the skies
The other dipping its wing into the sea of grass
The king of the field surveying all that is his once more
Then; dipping low towards the grass, disappears.
Swift.

Jack Watson (13)

All Wrapped Up . . .

He stood by the bar, in a nonchalant pose,
Confidence oozed from his head to his toes,
His ten gallon hat would only hold three.
He glared at the barman and ordered, 'Whiskey!'
On closer inspection those around him saw,
That in paper boots he stood on the floor,
His spurs didn't glitter, his spurs didn't spin,
When people look'd closer, they were paper thin.
His trousers of denim, a pale shade of blue,
His chaps held together with string and glue,
Yes, you've guessed it they too were paper made,
So was that hat, but it gave him some shade.
His shirt, a candy blue stripe without a collar,
His waistcoat, a brown paper wrapping colour,
His long johns, from a paper pattern made,
And a paper saddle by his feet was laid.
His horse was restrained with a paper bridle,
As it stood by the stables, looking quite idle,
That cowboy he'd drunk a bottle and more,
Before the bar-keep slung him out of the door.
The wind whipp'd around as he staggered along,
Bawdily reciting an insulting song,
The sheriff heard our cowboy a-cussing,
And arrested him . . . for simple rustling!

Helen Smith

The First Step

I wait till someone loves me
Reaches out to show they care
Just sit back to see if they
Really care I'm here

I wait and nothing happens
No one smiles or comes
To break their love into my world
To give me power to live my life

So, perhaps, I'll have to do the thing
Take the first step - smile or wave
Say 'hello' and 'weather is nice'
Their response is love, it came.

Pam Mills

Going To School
(Submitted by Cathy Mearman in loving memory of her grandfather.)

Going to school in a bus is great fun,
For it's easier far than having to run,
And if we are late, it is not our fault,
It's the poor old engine which had to halt.

Lessons at school now are really not bad,
In fact, there are plenty to make us glad.
We've each got a subject at which we shine,
If it's only the dinner we have at half-time.

Leaving the school at the end of term . . .
Will I finish with teachers, or cease to learn?
I think not, for if what I'm told is true,
Life's one long lesson for me and for you.

And going to school is only life's start
In teaching us all to play our own part.
There are some who must walk and others who run,
For there isn't a bus for everyone.

Coming at last, to the close of life's door . . .
D'you think that I'll ask for a few lessons more?
I may falter, O Master! I've only begun,
Though for me, 'twill be Heav'n, if I hear His 'Well done'.

Edwin V Atkinson

Untitled

Once upon a golden time many years ago,
There was a mansion called Golden Grove
There, they would help the sick and wounded
Voices, whispers, if only they could tell
The joys and woes of Golden Grove
Today the present, we will be back
Nursing the sick, injured and wounded
Healing the wounds . . . healing the wounds
The voices and whispers of the present
Will be heard . . . will be heard
Bring our heroes home, bring them home
Healing the wounds
Golden Grove we salute you.

Shirley McDonnell

Goodnight My Saviour
(Dedicated to Simon Moon)

Goodnight my saviour,
Sleep now.
Close your eyes and rest.
Dream of love and freedom,
Dream of life with no pain.

When you awake in the morning,
See me, touch me, smell me.
Feel my presence.

I'll be there if you want me.
I'll be there if you need me.
Never will I leave you,
Unless you tell me to go.

I still see your face in my mind.
Engraved is your name on my heart.
I'm trying my hardest not to push you away.
I'm holding on to the rope so tight.
It'll stop us from drifting, right?

Goodnight my saviour.
Sleep now.
You'll always be in my heart,
Even if I'm not in yours.

Natasha Joan Dono (15)

Eat Up Those Genetically Modified Greens My Lad!

I ate up all my greens, Mum
Just as you asked me to,
But I was wondering if it was
The clever thing to do.

My hair has turned a funny green
And looks like un-ripe wheat.
I've grown a finger on each foot,
My shoes won't fit my feet!

And when it's dark my nose glows red
Just like one of my eyes.
The other is a sombre grey,
Just like those new pork pies.

My friends all call me 'Mutant'.
It's a smashing new nickname.
Now that I've got a scaly neck
I'm apportioned lots of fame.

Another thing I'm chuffed about -
I'm no longer plagued by flies,
For everything within three feet
Drops dead before my eyes!

This really is quite fun you know,
I'm beginning to enjoy it.
If I can find my mouth sometime
I'm having 'seconds' of it!

James G Ryder

Passing Out

They march up and down in perfect time,
In their best pressed uniforms.
Rifles on shoulders, caps on head
With boots polished brighter than glass.
The weak winter sunshine glistens
From the prized regiment badges, worn so proudly.
Weeks of practice and training,
All for this one moment.

Their young faces, smooth and pale,
Set in serious concentration.
Counting their steps and turns in their heads.
For precision perfection.
Parents stand and cheer; applaud
And cry. The tears of pride, tinged with distant worry,
A sight for all to see.
Not hidden, no shame.

The mothers stand and smile,
Hiding their real thoughts,
Feeling the tear in her chest.
As the boy moves away
Into adulthood and independence.
My boy, she thinks, so smart
So grown up; now a man.
But still Mummy's special soldier.

And the fathers stand with mixed emotions.
Chests puffed like proud peacocks.
Their little boys have swapped toy guns
For real rifles, and the training to use them.
Hearts are fit to burst, plus envy
Of a son whose life of
Excitement and adventure is just beginning
And Daddy's protection is no longer needed.

Then the dismiss, and the whoops of joy.
Some boys run to their mothers
Others coolly swagger to waiting family.
They accept handshakes, slaps on the back
And lipstick kisses. Drinks are bought,
The alcohol ban has been lifted.
All worries of conflict to be faced are
Securely closeted for one day.

No reality today,
Just the pride of what the boy has achieved.

Joanne Lutwyche

Healing The Wounds

Lillian was born on a summer's day
Dick was born in the month of May
Instant love was in their eyes
As they told each other with mournful sighs
I love you till the end of time
Even though we don't have a dime
It was the war time you see
So Father had to run off reluctantly
Leaving Mother and me all alone
To fend for ourselves at home
Ammunition my mother made
While waiting to hear from the other side
What had happened to husband and Father dear
Always keeping a face of good cheer
Soon war had ended, the men returned home
Mother and Father stood all alone . . . with me, amen.

Glenys M Bowell

The Last Bomber

We were damaged over Dresden,
despatching our lethal load,
determined Hitler's factories . . .
. . . with bombs would be bestowed;
'Chantelle Baby' bore us,
how we put our trust in her,
this Lancaster belle,
if wearisome we were.
One engine hit,
we thought our time was due,
'Never again for England,
only the rare returning few',
a crew living on nerves,
black billowed from the port,
gunner Franks injured,
the Dover cliffs sought.

This was the last bomber,
the makings of the mission,
airmen victorious,
realising ambition,
Kent bound, amid the flames,
the sweat, blood, endeavour,
heroes - some didn't make it home,
all to be remembered forever.

Andrew Gruberski

My Child

In my heart
I hold,
Your heart,
Your soul,
Your every breath.
I hold,
You,
My child.

Clare Todd

A Hero's Cry

War knows sorrow and disgrace
It knows the horror
That shows on one's face
It is a horrible extreme
Where lives are lost
By people unseen
We see the carnage
The bloody, the bruised
The unfortunate and abused
The horrors and reality of it all
Are forever imprinted
On the souls of men
Crusaders, visionaries
Voices crying for justice and peace
Fighting a war
In this godforsaken place

Donna Louise Salisbury

No Time To Say Goodbye
(Dedicated to Andrew my nephew who we sadly lost to an rta)

I'm sat by myself,
Just wondering why, why me?
Sat by myself, by the sea.

Not a sound just the birds,
Flying up high, so high,
Wish I was a bird.

Why? Because then I could be,
In the sky,
Close by,
And ask why? Why me?

Why did we lose Andy?
He was free.
Wish I could see you once again,
To say goodbye, way up high.
Our lovely 19-year-old Andy.

Tracey Davies

I Sit At Night

I sit at night and think of all the fun I've had
And then I remember my long-lost friends, and this makes me feel so sad.

We started in the army when we were young, and full of fun.
When all we had to think of was the work we had done.
No thought of war, no thought of strife
We joined the army for a better life.

Then on an August in '69, we had the call to go
Not overseas, but to a place within our shores.
To Belfast we all gathered as trouble had arrived
To man the streets and keep the peace, this we had to strive.
When friends and neighbours, on the streets could not see eye to eye,
With bullets, bombs and beatings and people starting to die.

It was the British soldier sent to man the streets that day,
To try and sort the trouble out, but the people would not play.
But the government back home, that put their noses in,
And on the streets we soldiers thought this a sin.

The army was sent to do the job, that the police or others could not.
We were there, they were not, and this is what they forgot.
From the time we went to Ireland, to stop this bloody mess
The only recognition was a medal on our chest.

But the boys that did not make it, with their young lives taken away,
They have been forgotten by the kids that come out to play,
By the friends and neighbours from that place that could not see eye to eye.
They do not think of the soldiers, as their families say goodbye.

I sit at night and think of all the fun I've had
And then I remember my long-lost friends and this makes me feel so sad.
But they shall not be forgotten by us that served so well,
We will live our lives out, in our own living hell.

Arfon Williams Ex R R W (71)

The Traveller's Rest

Urban legends, village myths - what make you of these, my friend?
Tales spun into yarns of fear -
Mysteries and secrets left unclear,
So many stories swamped with eerie end.
This 'ere is no fairy fable, 'tis true as I am sound -
This inn I know of - edge of wooded lane,
Cobble-bricked and slated, ashen grey,
Standing dark 'gainst the silver moonlit clouds.
Dusted with a musty stench in pale oil-light,
A signpost o'er the heavy, oaken door -
'Travellers, do come in', it begs, for one and all.
Welcoming to weary men who need to stay the night.
And sleep they may, but where next morn are seen
These wandering drifters tired and worn?
Along with any sign or clear discern,
Of a tavern near the lane, amidst the trees.
You see, they say 'tis there one night, the next it's gone to nowt.
This dwelling with beds and sleepy vagrants bound,
Becomes illusory, spectral of its grounds,
'Til next it appears in darkened night, when no one is about.
Ah! Simple disappearance! Humours me to laugh into my ale!
Rumours of the arty gypsy tongue -
To note and heed such mock is wrong.
It stands as always, staid in vision - old and real.
So, if you ever pass this country stead, I beg you be my guest.
Ignore the tales to scare ye off, 'tis only hamlet hearsay.
Be sure a welcome here, my friend - any night upon your way,
And don't hesitate for lodgings at my inn, 'The Traveller's Rest'.

Lynda Ann Green

Rugby Forever A Beautiful Game

Rugby plays with a funny shaped ball
Going any direction if at all
A contact sport, of that no doubt, the boys giggling, a shield
Of dressing room culture, that transmits to the field
Commentators orgasmic, when players, are crushed to the ground
Enjoy the pouring of blood, battered bruising making a sound
Calls for return of rucking, with painful marks carved out with stud
Same breath, complain high injury count made in mud
Blaming the broken young men, for related loss of form
It is a game that falls to the ground in ways that are torn
Proud talk of honesty, integrity and respect
Yet those speaking to inspire litter the video, dressing room, playing field, using foul language direct
Offending a desire, for the family game, best seated in main stand
Cheating is accepted, cheating when unseen, is clever trickery -
Taking off his head, slightly high, amounts to jiggery pokery
Play the referee, cut corners, professional foul
Repeated offence, 'Go talk to your players.'
'I will,' you lie!
Meanwhile, deep in the dark world of scrum nobody knows
The opposing lump may give rise to abuse
With elongated heads, squeezed testicles, earlobe misuse
They bear down, interlocking, sweating, with driving muscles
The referee rightly decides rightly whose turn it is,
Better the home side get the call
The main man needing to live out the night overall
Listens to the baying crowd
Fans bored with the game, likely hissing, booing, jeering, beer well shifted
With Mexican wave, jumping up and down in turn, with arms uplifted
Or fight through occupied, packed seats, towards bars or loos
Replenish alcohol or p**s water on bystanders' shoes
At its best, the game remains a passion which ignites and excites
As defences get stronger, getting to the line much harder
Going over, when it comes is all that smarter
Watching the magic of Shane Williams' speed of foot, dancing,
Side stepping, thrills and makes you cry
Rugby forever a beautiful game, culminating as it does in a try.

Ron Constant

Observations Of Being

Do you really know who you are?
Are you fully aware that when you go
There will never be another quite the same?
And when it cuts to the bone,
Remember
That while flesh yields,
Time heals.
Though the scars remain they will
Weave themselves into the pattern of your being -
You are unique,
Marked, magnificent and transformed,
Resplendent in conquered pain.
The chains that bind will break,
Be free, take flight -
Transcend into glory.

Tara NíBhroin Byrne

The Explosion

It wasn't Hiroshima or Nagasaki
A tender flower, serene rivulet
The soft glow of moon
Yet it exploded
Massacring the emotions
Rooting out love, love

Your words like atomic bomb
Dropped in this heart
Extinguished smile, smile
And teardrops rained

I am the skeleton of love

Put me in your museum
And visit my corpse
Each explosive decade

Arun Budhathoki

War Poem

We didn't want this war -
but once it started we all got drawn in.
The storyline is simple - the action -
almost complete. The long race for their capital
or any city, save that it's not ours, that's too scary -
I mean how real do we want reality TV?
Some guy said the Gulf War didn't happen,
Iraq, Vietnam, The Somme, Waterloo, Hastings and all
holding the shield wall,
under the hoar apple tree, King Harold's eye,
we watched it all on Sky, each episode
flicking between what they say of the past,
and what they say we now should feel
about this eternal film reel, running on and on,
this is a war that can't be won: it's never done.

We were all looking out for special effects
American explosions, cool British grit,
clean, fresh, digitised -
those extras crowding round a water pipe
till our friends said that their friends said
they knew the grieving family, the lost daughter, the dead son.
But that didn't change our lives at all.
Put the set on, stare at the wall -
that dusty supermarket of boxed bones,
twenty years old, with confidential records,
luggage notes that silently try to tell
tear-stained families about this dry hell.

Relatives, milling about, dazed,
bringing home their loved ones from a hole in the sand,
seeing them as they never thought to see
tightly rolled in their material essences, clutched in hugs,
green skulls and long shanks wrapped in tatty rugs
handed back fleshless like so much lost property.

Christopher J P Smith

Out Of The Everyday

He and I were sitting in the car,
Silent and still,
Waiting for Alex.
Gentle, ordinary afternoon, cloudy . . .
Children were unhurriedly
Coming out of school.

In front of us, a patch of grass -
A young hedgehog unexpectedly appeared.
This was just . . . beautiful.
Confidently it was going fast,
Its long, thin legs
Often changing direction.

It soon chose to cross the road,
It aimed for the road,
Going so fast in no time
It was in danger.
We just . . . stayed there, sitting,
Passively watching, worried -
            Should we . . . ?

A woman driver was behind a parked car,
Waiting for a chance to move on.
So little time was needed
For the hedgehog to reach the pavement.
It decided to stop,
Suddenly, under one of her wheels.

Perfectly hidden, perfectly tranquil.
In that dark place, a dark, lonely place -
            Should we . . . ?
It happened so quickly.
From life to death -
She moved on, then she was gone.
In an instant of nothing.

Claire-Lyse Sylvester

The Letter . . .

Today I got the letter
I knew that he had wrote
I knew it would be full of love
a lump rose in my throat

I opened it in silence
a teardrop, then a sigh
it was his thoughts for us at home
in the event that he should die

He told us to be strong and proud
and remember him with fun
and not to dwell upon the fact
he'd died by the enemy's gun

The army was his joy, his life
it was all he wanted to be
a soldier, proud and strong and true
he hoped that we would see . . .

He'd lived the dream, achieved his goal
he hoped not all in vain
and we should all remember that
whenever we spoke his name

The letter now is wet and blurred
and I can begin to see
my soldier died, *a hero*
but he's still just, 'my boy' to me.

Amanda Crowden

No Canadian Picnic

Two boys, a rough Australian and I,
On some Albertan hillside years ago,
Paired up with girls. One was a sweetie-pie
Or Aussie Fred's. She had a friend in tow
Brought to romance me. Fred had planned it so.

The sun was hot. My prospect smouldered there,
Not saying much but giving me the eye.
So packed with western promise was her stare
That some might have surrendered with a sigh
But somehow my 'Hello' came out 'Goodbye.'

No chance of keeping mum what happened then.
Fred loved to tell a tale against his mate.
'This Pom was off inside a count of ten.
That's hardly dinkum on a double date.
I'd fixed him up - 'e 'ad it on a plate!'

The lads near died with laughing as he'd drawl
'These uppish Pommie toffs are all the sime.
He gave this sheila no good marks at all,
Just eyes 'is watch (Fred hams the heavy mime)
And sez, 'Ho, goodness me, is thet the time?'

And then he's gone and running down the slope
While I'm left fighting off the eager squaws,
Man-eaters both. I didn't 'ave a 'ope . . . '
No arguing with Aussie Fred because
The swine is telling it just like it was.

Ian Rae

Higher Irlam Old Cottages

Do you remember the cottages where the library now stands?
There were 5 or 6 on this land
At the side of No 1 Hurst Fold
A post office full of gold
Outside a small park where my nanny did sit
After taking a drink 'The Nag's Head' only a bit.

The cottage a two up, two down
Now no longer seen in this town
Knock on the door and enter in
A world so small but free from sin
Elsie and Frank lived here quite a while
Until demolition then there was no smile.

We all remember the days sat by a log fire
The games and the fun we never did tire
Frank would come home from a long day of toil
To our secret hiding place he would foil
Occasionally the spools for a cinema show
Often seeing the trains whilst the whistle did blow.

Into the kitchen Elsie would go
I would follow ever so slow
For there in the pantry a cobweb or two
Small and large but no spider in view
Out came the stone bottle full of ginger beer
Was there refusal, no fear.

As 7.30 arrived it was time to go home
Elsie would walk us so we didn't roam
Occasionally we'd stay and all sleep in one room
As Nanny had the other, it was as small as a broom.

The loo was outside down the path in the yard
When it was cold the journey was hard
A wooden bench with a hole in the middle
Newspaper hung whilst one played the fiddle.

The yard was shared by the neighbours in line
No one minded, everything seemed fine
No garage was had as Elsie and gang
Would travel if anywhere in the sharabanc.

Where the bathroom was I didn't think
I only had a wash in the sink
A tin bath sat in the outhouse
Was the water shared by man and spouse?

UNITED IN INSPIRATION - The Golden Grove Appeal Poetry Collection

No room for a cooker, the kitchen was small
Stairs in the middle, no space for a hall
A dishwasher, a dryer, Elsie wouldn't understand
Only a dollytub, mangle passed through her hand.

Elsie's cooking was done on the stove by the fire
Her fresh bread and cakes today would inspire
Eggs were collected from the hens in the run
Frank brought home wood so the fire would burn like the sun.

No carpets, as the floor was flagged
Sometimes through the house coal was dragged
Coats were hung as you walked in the door
Very carefully so they didn't fall on the floor.

The lights were dim and had a strange smell
For electricity in this house did not dwell
Wallpaper, paint were not a part
As artex walls looked quite smart.

Frank rolled his own but often smoked a pipe
We collected brambles in August when ripe
Elsie would add apple and bake us a pie
Her recipe I can't beat however I try.

When it came time for the cottages to be pulled down
Elsie, Frank and Nanny were sent to the far side of town
Too far now for my nanny to walk
And sit in the pub with her friends for a talk.

Slowly my nanny found it too difficult to move
And one day from this Earth she was removed
This then made her room empty and free
So there I lived for a year until Mike married me.

Tripe and onions was their favourite meal
Today all this seems so unreal
It was long ago and now in the past
But with me these memories will last.

Sandra Moran

Beautiful Wales

I look for tranquility in the depth of my mind
And often float back to the time of my youth
Not to my parents or the house where I lived
But to the mountains of Wales in search of the truth

And here is where I find the true beauty of Wales
The depth of her valleys and pastures so green
A walk in the mountain, wild flowers and wind
Such is the beauty, what a wonderful scene

Lose yourself in the hills and in your thoughts
And modern society will be cleansed from your mind
For the beautiful surroundings in the valleys of green
Are for me at this moment, just a distant dream

Richard Jones

Christmas Truce 1914

Beside this filthy, rat-filled trench we stand,
Obeying orders. For, upon this day
There must be peace on Earth. The guns lie still
And foes hold hands - as brothers.
Husbands reach out to husbands, sons to sons,
In bold defiance of the wanton rules of war.
The dullness of our senses breeds contempt
For fragile peace that passes with the dawn.
We lift our eyes to Heaven and dread new days
When memories of comradeship lie dead.
Restoration of dissent brings anguish. Fresh orders now.
Along the Western Front the carnage must continue.
Machine guns stutter - weary mortals hobble on
Cursing the crude absurdity of war.

Eirlys Jones

UNITED IN INSPIRATION - The Golden Grove Appeal Poetry Collection

Treasured Memories

Glimpses of my childhood sometimes flit into my head
Stirred by a sight or sound or something I have read
The cottage at the foot of the hill is where I'm meant to be
As memories of my family come floating back to me

The rooms hold many secrets of many years ago
With thick old walls so stout and strong and beamed ceiling so low
The glow of the flickering fire on a sleepy winter's night
Lighting the old dark room with warmth and flickering light

Outside the air feels frosty and cold upon my nose
It was important to wrap up warm from head right to our toes
On the clothes line in the small back yard icicles softly sway
Soft patterns form on the windows which remain from night to day

But inside the cat is sitting purring as sleepy as can be
And grandparents gently snoring watched by Mum and me
My thoughts now turn to summer, long days filled with summer sun
My sister hiding in the coal shed having lots of fun

Grandad's lovely roses caught the eye of passers-by
While I sat on the front doorstep watching clouds up in the sky
The days seemed long and happy and cares seemed far away
Those hours spent with my family I remember to this day

Then suddenly it's over and here I am again
Back in the present day standing in the rain
But then I smile as I remember my blessings many fold
I now have my own loving family to love as I grow old

Gillian Todd

A Steamy Dream

The station's throng hums quite a buzz, as they see the sight in front of us
We cannot help but stop and stare - at the beautiful lady standing there
Her elegant poise and graceful lines remind us all of happier times
With gleaming paint and shining brass this stylish lady oozes class
Her motions, slides and shapely rods, caressingly oiled by men with cloths

Final checks are now complete so we board the train and take our seats
The fingers on the terminal clock, indicate it's time we're off
Her whistle sounds and she summons her strength -
Then she eases away with our train of great length

The fireman shovels jet-black coal in her white hot firebox hole
He starts to feel her searing heat, but her appetite he has to meet
He's no time to take his seat - he's light and dancing on his feet
The driver's gaze fixed straight ahead, likes the signals green not red
Her regulator he keeps gripping to stop her mighty wheels from slipping

Our lady quickly gathers speed, we're moving very swift indeed
We feel her power and hear her beat, her exhaust note sings clear and sweet
Now we face a lengthy climb, we wonder can she keep to time
She raises the echoes and shatters the peace -
The air all around taints with sulphur and grease

A cacophony from her chimney's roar, like Danté's Inferno she spits sparks galore
The driver whispers in her ear, 'Come on my lovely, you're getting near'
As pistons chatter with billowing steam our regal lady reigns supreme
With '14 on' and steam to spare, we share her joy beyond compare!

She thunders onwards through the night, under the glow of her firebox light
Her whistle's shrill and piercing scream, abruptly wakes us from our dream
We then reflect in retrospect on things that might have been
Did it happen, was it true . . . that decision we leave to you!

Gary K Raynes

Death's Silence

Sleep now, rest your head
Stay with the angels, let yourself be led
To a place where you, can finally live free
And see all the things, you never got to see

The things you wished for, things you dreamt
Be the person you never could, your ageing now exempt
To fly, to soar, the distance now obsolete
To fulfill your life, until the time we meet

And once again, we'll be face to face
To be accompanied by your embrace
To watch you laugh, watch you smile
And without any problem, overcome any trial

You may be gone, but to me you still live
Because even in memory, you still give
The greatest warmth, the happiest feeling
Which in times of sadness, provide the best healing

You always made me happy, never made me sad
Somehow seemed to pick me up, when things felt bad
Always knew just what to say, and always what to do
But I guess that comes, from being the person that is you

Every morning now, I look at making it through the date
Always holding my head high, refuse to procrastinate
Never will I worry, about how things turned out
Always hold such hope in my heart, never any doubt

It'll be a while, before I'm stood at the gate
We all know death's coming, it's in our fate
But at least I know, down deep in my heart
I've lived my life to the fullest, right from the start

I'll see you again my friend, but until that day
There's only so much that I can say
I love you and I miss you, with every new moon
Goodbye to you . . . . I'll see you soon

Michael James Ryan

Two Men Singing

Grass stems clasp themselves round my ankles
As if to brace my unsteady gaze.
Every blade growing on these high hills
Knows I won't look down upon the waves.

The sea crashing rhythmically into the rocky shore,
One of nature's soothing sounds,
Is silenced within me by a noisy inner roar,
Pulse rising, my blood pressure pounds.

Feeling so exposed, so elevated with only sky up top,
I'm held fast to where I stand, afraid that I might fall.
All that's between that keeps me from a terrible drop
Is this stony cliff-side band of tumble down wall.

Held immovable in the clutches of my fear,
I'm frozen solid in its icy-hot embrace.
So still am I, that ambling sheep draw near,
Sensing no threat to browse this lofty space.

Survival screams for me to come away from the edge,
Abandon this quest to walk at dangerous heights!
Heed the worried voice telling you to leave the ledge.
Leave it to gulls and to ravens to attempt such flights.

Only the captain of a ship should stand at its helm,
Anyone else and the whole of it will doubtless list.
Better for you to keep to the beaten path, a safer realm,
Familiar ground, known terrain with lesser risk.

Too frightened to raise my head to scan the ocean below,
So removed from that experience called 'belonging'
Beyond the touch of this scene's beauty, I'm just about to go.
Staying only to ponder if I'm doing the wrong thing,

There comes to my ears from some far distant source,
Carried by the wind, brought on the wings of a dove,
The faintest strains of a tune sung with mystical force,
Drift forth across the waters, as if from the heavens above.

This light-hearted murmur rises to the top of the hill.
Caressing my senses like an invisible mist of notes
A duet with such magical powers to invade the will,
The melody's origin is two men singing in a boat.

Forgetting my dread, I strain to hear more clearly,
Captivated by their hearty voices, music to my ears.
The spell they weave, done with words, not merely,
For no simple ditty could so dispel such dark fears.

Listening to that merry chorus, soon I begin to feel
At last my own ship's sailing. Why cling to the mast?
Spirits restored, not caring if this change in me is real,
With toes tapping, fingers snapping, my spirit soars at last.

I'd join these singers in their song but I mustn't intrude,
So I hum praises for their wizardry that unbound my feet
Their happy tune, a gift to me received with gratitude
Braces me along the way, as I dance among the sheep.

Isolde Nettles Mackay

Forever Mine

You see my every movement
When I'm here, by night or day,
Your expression never changes,
To any other way.

You watch me while undressing,
And fall wearily to bed,
Where, sunken in a pillow,
Is my silent dreaming head.

Whatever I may say to you,
Your answer is but nil,
Whether sleeping or awaking,
You just watch, and listen still.

You never frown or question,
You smile . . . but never laugh,
But, I know you're mine forever,
Here . . . in this photograph!

Helen Richards

Heroes Retreat

The wind whispers gently thro' the huge rustling trees,
The large herd of deer graze silently in the parkland below.
Peace and tranquillity puts one completely at ease
To wander at your leisure at one pace . . . that's slow,
Thro' the gates all rusted, down the drive so worn,
There stands proud and magnificent with clock tower so tall,
Gelli Aur . . . Golden Grove . . . looking oh so forlorn,
So cold empty and neglected yet welcoming us all.

What's going on behind those smiling eyes,
As we welcome them all home with pride,
The noise . . . the heat . . . the dust . . . he cries,
The taste of death on his lips . . . the horrors of war taken in his stride,
So surely we owe them much more don't you think,
More recognition, understanding, respect and support,
They are our heroes, each one, but lost in a blink,
So please, pause for a moment and give them a thought.

Old veterans, young military their experiences talk free,
The torment, the anger, the doubt,
The invisible wounds that no one can see,
Each knowing exactly what it's all about,
The young and the old all damaged by war,
The doors will be open whenever you fall,
Gelli Aur, perfection like nowhere before,
Will heal all your wounds, just give us a call.

Jane Green

UNITED IN INSPIRATION - The Golden Grove Appeal Poetry Collection

Forward Poetry Information

We hope you have enjoyed reading this book - and that you will continue to enjoy it in the coming years.

If you like reading and writing poetry drop us a line, or give us a call, and we'll send you a free information pack.

Alternatively if you would like to order further copies of this book or any of our other titles, then please give us a call or log onto our website at www.forwardpoetry.co.uk

Forward Poetry Information
Remus House
Coltsfoot Drive
Peterborough
PE2 9JX
(01733) 890099